Sacred Rites

Some Other Titles from Falcon Press

Antero Alli
  Angel Tech: A Modern Shaman's Guide to Reality Selection
  Angel Tech Talk (audio)
  The Eight-Circuit Brain
  State of Emergence
  Experiential Astrology
  The Akashic Record Player
Christopher S. Hyatt, Ph.D. & Antero Alli
  A Modern Shaman's Guide to a Pregnant Universe
Christopher S. Hyatt, Ph.D.
  Undoing Yourself with Energized Meditation and Other Devices
  To Lie Is Human: Not Getting Caught Is Divine
  Secrets of Western Tantra: The Sexuality of the Middle Path
  Hard Zen, Soft Heart
Christopher S. Hyatt, Ph.D. with contributions by
  Wm. S. Burroughs, Timothy Leary, Robert Anton Wilson et al.
  Rebels & Devils: The Psychology of Liberation
S. Jason Black and Christopher S. Hyatt, Ph.D.
  Pacts with the Devil: A Chronicle of Sex, Blasphemy & Liberation
  Urban Voodoo: A Beginner's Guide to Afro-Caribbean Magic
Peter J. Carroll
  The Chaos Magick Audios
  PsyberMagick
Phil Hine
  Condensed Chaos: An Introduction to Chaos Magic
Joseph Lisiewski, Ph.D.
  Kabbalistic Handbook for the Practicing Magician
Israel Regardie
  The Complete Golden Dawn System of Magic
  The Golden Dawn Audios
Denny Sargent
  Naga Magick: The Wisdom of the Serpent Lords
Steven Heller
  Monsters & Magical Sticks: There's No Such Thing as Hypnosis?

For up-to-the-minute information on prices and availability, please visit our website at
originalfalcon.com

SACRED RITES

Journal Entries of a Gnostic Heretic

by
ANTERO ALLI
& Guests of Honor

Preface by
Geri De Stefano-Webre

THE *Original* FALCON PRESS
TEMPE, ARIZONA, U.S.A.

Copyright © 2023 C.E. by Antero Alli

All rights reserved. No part of this book, in part or in whole, may be reproduced, transmitted, or utilized, in any form or by any means, electronic or mechanical, including photocopying, recording, or by any information storage and retrieval system, without permission in writing from the publisher, except for brief quotations in critical articles, books and reviews.

International Standard Book Number: 978-1-61869-954-1
ISBN: 978-1-61869-955-8 (mobi)
ISBN: 978-1-61869-956-5 (ePub)
Library of Congress Catalog Card Number: 2023934483

First Edition 2023
Second Edition 2023

Front Cover by Jonathan Delaney Marsh
Photographic Art by Antero Alli

The paper used in this publication meets the minimum requirements of the American National Standard for Permanence of Paper for Printed Library Materials Z39.48-1984

Address all inquiries to:
The Original Falcon Press
1753 East Broadway Road #101-277
Tempe, AZ 85282 U.S.A.
(or)
PO Box 3540
Silver Springs NV 89429 U.S.A.

website: originalfalcon.com
email: info@originalfalcon.com

Dedicated to

Those amplified souls
Radiating transmissions of freedom,
Find the others, see them, be seen!
Celebrate your electromagnetic dreams.

acknowledgements

Since 1977, several hundred individuals from all walks of life have participated in this Paratheatre medium, each one bringing their own distinct influence into the work, sometimes shaping its next developing direction. In this incomplete list of past participants <u>underlined</u> names have completed two or more Labs (of 5 to 20 weeks each) while the rest have undergone at least one Lab and/or a Weekend Intensive with me. I remain grateful for the presence of and the work accomplished by each and every one. — Antero Alli

<u>Sylvi Alli</u> – <u>Nick Walker</u> – <u>Ed Welsh</u> – <u>Maple Holmes</u> – <u>Memorie Eden</u> – <u>Lindsay Reich</u> – <u>Bryan Smith</u> – Hank Peterson – Wendy Allegaert – <u>LD McClure</u> – <u>Patton Small</u> – <u>Jogen Salzberg</u> – <u>Maggie Medlin</u> – <u>Kisei Costenbader</u> – <u>Helia Rasti</u> – <u>Cibyl Kavan</u> – <u>Miriam Sluis</u> – <u>Julian Simeon</u> – <u>Robin Coomer</u> – <u>Alaska Yamada</u> – <u>Brian Livingston</u> – <u>Jote Mahern</u> – <u>Utam Moses</u> – <u>Trey Donovan</u> – <u>Jennifer Bruce</u> – Kajanne Pepper – <u>Nathan Rosquist</u> – <u>Alanna Williams</u> – <u>Jaya Miller</u> – <u>Justin Palermo</u> – <u>Paradox Pollack</u> – <u>David Hunt</u> – <u>Arun Ragan</u> – <u>Sage Reilly</u> – <u>Jessie Drake</u> – Jackson Parker – <u>Robert D'Esposito</u> – <u>Lily Gael</u> – <u>Brandt Stickley</u> – <u>Lesley Beth</u> – <u>Wes Matusewicz</u> – <u>James L. Wagner</u> – Kathleen Terese O'Brian – Abby Dahlquist – Travis Wheeler – Mathew Cichon – Maggie Medlin – Abigail Waterman – Amy Sprengelmeyer – <u>Matteo Jaffe</u> – <u>Liam Carey</u> – <u>JoJo Razor</u> – <u>Madeline H.D. Brown</u> – <u>Justin Gordon</u> – <u>Jenny Logico</u> – <u>Baptiste Andre</u> – <u>Crystal Cobra Faerie</u> – <u>Mahipal Lunia</u> – <u>Sergey Berezin</u> – <u>John M. Doyle</u> – <u>Camille M. Hildebrandt</u> – <u>Andrew Reichart</u> – <u>Lori Salomon</u> – <u>Joshua Bewig</u> – <u>Marianne Shine</u> – <u>Adam Palermo</u> – <u>Todd Richmond</u> – <u>Michael Davenport</u>

– Brendan Ramsden – Gabriel Dietz – Jonathan Delaney Marsh – Douglas Allen – Elijah Parizhsky – Jadina Lilien – Martin Muller – Ian Brooks – Jeri Preston – Scott Kirchenbaum – Karen Thurber – Barbara Martin – Opal Essence – Jessie Woletz – Sean Herbert – Victoria Ziemba – Nita Bryant – Darius Sohel – Daniel Larlham – Faye Dylan – Lisa Wells –– Joseph Bailey –– Starlette Nite – Vix Vixen – Vincent Tamer – Todd Dickerson – Joy Mazzola – Jessica Bockler – Matthew Purdon – Kate Gibson – Lloyd Bricken – Gavin Wittje – Chela Farrar – Benny Sadeh – Christine Benvenuto – Tamuz Shiran – Tom Westin – Carole Swann – Ishmael Aylwin Mcintosh – Kim Criswell – Venee Call-Ferrer – Frank Janzad – Amy Marks – Felecia Faulkner – Lauren Raine – Duncan Cook – Brian Jenkins – Wendy Vastine – Leah Kahn – Lea Bender – Linda Rose – Lissa Ivy – Finley Kipp – Elan Dia – Masuda Jamshid – Diarmid Baillie – Heather Hanan – Kyra Auerbach – Troy Skeels – Desmonde Daisy – Oliver Crow – Jonathon Furst – Jane De Cuir – Tom Evanoff – Serene Zloof – Brian Jenkins – Alan Brinson – Nathaniel Taylor – John Chung – Christa Ray – Jakob Bokulich – Benjamin Jarrett – Paula Curry – Julie B. Oak – Jonnie Gilman – Joy Shayne Laughter – Richard Bradshaw – Onnah Sisk – Theresa Laughinghare – Zoe Alowan – Kathy Ketman – Lily Nova – Ambe Ray – Olga Kupriyanova – Seamus Qin – Jadina Lilien – Jeffrey Danese – Lapo – Bob Jensen – Marit Elverland – Gavin Ropke – Donald DeWitt – David Favor – Kenny Telesco – Steven Miller – Annie Bones – Marganne Hesch – Sima Wolf – Ray Turchetti – Benjamin Di Gregorio – Leslie Mahler – Steven Pitts – Susan Park – Douglass Truth – Kalina Wilson – Deanna Anderson – Jessica Kluess – Andrew Waitley – Joshua Leavitt – Seijun Yanagida – Sandy Lawrie – Brandt Stickely – Randal S. Slager – Fred Curchack's 1982 Mime class @ Sonoma State University – Esalen Institute Big Sur, 1986 – Naropa Institute, Boulder CO, 1987–88

Who was she who made love to you
in your dream, while you slept?

Where do the things in dreams go?
Do they pass to the dreams of others?

And does the father who lives in your dreams
die again when you awaken?

In dream, do plants blossom
and their solemn fruit ripen?

Pablo Neruda,
from "The Book of Questions"

Table of Contents

Preface
by Geri De Stefano-Webre *15*

Genesis

Introduction *20*
Paratheatre, active imagination, the asocial climate

"Crux of the Matter" Interview *29*
When non-sectarian crucifixion archetypes get personal

The Ritual Journals
Antero Alli, Berkeley CA, 2000–2011 .... *43*

The Dreaming Ritualis Lab *44*
Choreographies created from movements recalled from dreams

The Aanima/Animus Lab, Spring 2001 .... *54*
Soul-retrieval rituals for reclaiming psychic projections

The Ancestors' Lab—Autumn 2001 .... *64*
Tapping ancestral wellsprings for guidance and healing

The Holy Trinity Lab—Autumn 2002 .... *83*
Excavating a triptych of sustaining core values

The Initiations Lab *87*
From initiatic experience to performance: "Orphans of Delirium"

Two-Faced Clowns Lab—Fall 2005 .... *97*
Developing a ritual clown show that suddenly turned serious

The "Song & Prayer Lab" Autumn 2006 .... *104*
"Whereabouts Unknown": our only public lab witnessing

The Chakra Lab—Spring 2007 .... *108*
Sourcing the Body's verticality of eight energy centers

Dreaming Ritual Lab—Spring 2008 .... *115*
Working within the dreaming vortex of the mountain

The Muses Lab—Spring 2010 .... *120*
Ritual dialogue with the elusive Muses archetype

Ritual Actions of the Muses Lab *128*
Advanced paratheatre methods with the Muses dialogue

The Journals of Others
Trained in this Paratheatre Medium *139*

The Anima/Animus Lab, 2001
    Serene Zloof *140*

"Orphans of Delirium", 2004
    Paradox Pollack *143*

"Orphans of Delirium", 2004
    Jakob Bokulich *145*

"Orphans of Delirium", 2004 Performance/Video
    Production Notes by Antero *148*

Technique Lab Reports, Spring 2005
    Leah Kahn, John M. Doyle, Sylvi Alli *150*

Alchemy Lab Reports, Spring 2006
    Nick Walker, Sylvi Alli, Jessica Bockler, & JoJo Razor *154*

Beginner's Mind Lab Reports, Fall 2007
    David Hunt, Jessie Woletz, Brendan Ramsden *163*

The Dreaming Ritual Lab, Winter 2008
    Sylvi Alli *171*

The Muses Lab, Spring 2010
    James Wagner *175*

Weekend Intensives
Outline of Ritual Structures, Designs, and Methods...................................*179*

The Portland Productions (2016–2018)
Notes on Pre-Production Labs and Performance Rituals........................*183*
  Living Rituals Dressed Up As Experimental Theatre..........................*184*
  "A Turbulence of Muses" – poetry by Arthur Rimbaud......................*185*
  "Bardoville" – poetry by Charles Bukowski (reviewed).....................*187*
  "Soror Mystica" – poetry by Hilda Doolittle (reviewed).....................*196*
  "Fallen Monsters" – poetry by William Blake..*203*
  "Escape from Chapel Perilous" – poetry by Sylvia Plath....................*208*
  The Celebrants – A Paratheatrical Video Experiment.........................*211*
  Film Review by David Finkelstein, Lake Ivan Film Journal...............*212*

  About the Author...*217*

PREFACE
by Geri De Stefano-Webre

When Antero sent me the typescript of *Sacred Rites* I found myself taking a sharp inhale of breath. Like one who might have been on the verge of drowning, lungs full of water. Gasping. Memory takes me to the times he made an appearance in my world. Each time heralded by some synchronic event that would inevitably result in a bruising, outside shock. Result: more dis-integration! Thank the gods! I can only hope for more.

I wondered, after these many years of no contact, what bit of magic and alchemy this sorcerer had up his sleeve now? His Presence was, is, and always will be, about offering one the opportunity to put oneself to death. Let it go. Go deeper. Being anywhere near him is a free dive into psyche. Silent. Scary. Satisfying when you know that another bit is cast off, revealing a pearl of greater or lesser price. Doesn't matter.

Antero and I have been working on similar ideas though, from very different perspectives. Recently, in the Work I do, I found myself annoyed with how it was going with students and the complications of working with a group spread out all over the globe via virtual class space. I knew enough to come back to myself for the answers and not blame anyone or any conditions and circumstances that were all too easy to target.

And there, in Antero's "Introduction" to *Sacred Rites,* were the words that needed saying, and the stark reminder of why we do the Work we do: an abiding curiosity as to the "whatness" of humanity, but specifically ourselves. What are we *really* up to and why? What is enslaving us? Or numbing us out so completely that we are perpetually on automatic? Quidditas?!

And, what are we willing to sacrifice, and what price are we willing to pay for our autonomy and freedom?

Antero is one of those rare Humans capable of "original thinking." This is only possible when you have the, no: not courage, but are driven by the realization of the terror of your situation. Soren Kierkegaard, in *"Fear and Trembling"* mapped it out quite clearly: you've come to the abyss. You can't go back, and you have no clue as to what lies on the other side. You're left with, what Antero describes as the "crux": that part of the journey that is the most difficult, treacherous.

Yes, there's choice: stop. Stay in the crux with the possibility of death, no return, or retrace your steps and start again or, in a state of terror and "I don't know" you take a leap into the unknown. Alli has shown us how to leap and how to trust.

Sacred Rites is a journal of the ideas, experiments and personal challenges Antero and his partner, Sylvi, undertake in their commitment to live their art. It is tantalizingly provocative, scary in the extreme, playful, deep, and in the end, there are no words in our limited vocabulary capable of truly conjuring up the depth of experience that Alli and the band of courageous participants, embark upon and begin to embody.

Gurdjieff's axiom: *Remember yourself,* is brought from thinking concept to a state of objective reality in this decades-long experiment into what it is to be a Human. Sacred Ritual/Sacred Dances: the

Sacred Rites

process of manifesting the Word, not through the mental masturbating mind, but through the rawness of the unknown body.

Alli journals this process unflinchingly. His missteps, and ecstatic states on equal footing. It's uncommon and rare for us to be brought into the intimate processes of ego-death and humility charted by an artist: to be shown the demons within and the journey into the verticality of God/love that, curiously, IS the ground we walk on. Alli shares it all: not caring what we might think as he's clearly comfortable in his skin.

Antero Alli is providing us with, not breadcrumbs to follow to the gingerbread house in the woods, but fucking boulders and flashing sign posts for anyone who has the courage and willingness to be, perhaps, insane, to truly

Remember themselves.

— Geri De Stefano-Webre, Ph.D.,
Transpersonal Consultant,
Vancouver B.C. Canada

GENESIS
Author Introduction &
The Crux Lab Interview
Turning Points & Developments in this Paratheatre Medium

Introduction
Paratheatre, Active Imagination, the Asocial Climate

Between 1977 and 2019, I have been developing a "paratheatre" medium (a term coined by Polish theatre director Jerzy Grotowski), combining methods of physical theatre, modern dance, vocalization, and standing Zazen to access the internal landscape of forces in the Body—*the impulses, emotions, sensations, tensions, and other autonomous forces*—towards their spontaneous expression in movement, vocal creations, symbolic gesture, characterization, and asocial interplay. These group ritual dynamics were explored in primarily asocial, non-performance-oriented "Labs" with occasional community outreaches in lecture-demos and experimental theatre productions, all under the umbrella of **ParaTheatrical ReSearch.**

Over four decades, several hundred individuals participated in this work (Berkeley CA, Boulder CO, Seattle WA, and Portland OR) with about 80% occurring behind closed doors in complete privacy, without audiences. During this four-decade era, thirteen public productions were staged: *"William Blake's Songs of Innocence and Experience" (1977),"Coronation at Stillnight" (1978), "The Conjunction" (1979), "Bring Out the Dead" (1988), "Mass of the Iconoclasts" (1992), "Orphans of Delirium" (2004), "Requiem for a Friend" (2005), "Songs as Vehicles" (2005), "A Turbulence of Muses" (2016), "Bardoville"* and *"Soror Mystica" (2017), "Fallen Monsters"* and *"Escape from Chapel Perilous" (2018).*

Sacred Rites

All public productions, lecture-demos, and private ritual labs ceased after Autumn Equinox, 2019. Why did I stop? After forty-two years, it felt like I had gone as far as I could go. Or maybe it was a prescient move to quit six months before the Covid pandemic hit. In a very personal way, this work never stopped. The long-term effects of so much immersion in these processes remains active in me daily. Once certain doors have been opened, they can't really shut again. No-Form, Verticality, Sourcing...

Active Imagination, the Self, and the Asocial

In our paratheatrical research, the physical body is posited as *an embodiment of the so-called Subconscious Mind.* With its complex webbing of bio-systems—*circulatory, skeletal, cellular, muscular, endocrine, etc.*—invisible to the naked eye of the conscious ego. This Paratheatre mirrors Carl Jung's method of "active imagination" for *making the unconscious, conscious* in a nonverbal, highly visceral, and physically active approach to accessing what Jung calls *the centralizing archetype of The Self,* representing the unified unconsciousness *and* consciousness of an individual with the Ego as a subservient subset of The Self.

This chiefly group-oriented process is neither social nor antisocial but *asocial.* Neither antisocial or social, *asocial* refers to a third point beyond the social/antisocial dichotomy. This Paratheatre medium is not set up to meet common social needs such as gaining emotional support from others, peer approval, courtship, friendship, and a sense of belonging in a community. Though these social needs are important to daily life situations, they can also impede and frustrate the spontaneous, creative response essential to Paratheatre work.

An asocial climate is initiated by realizing one's non-responsibility to others in the workspace where participants also agree to accept full accountability for their own safety and creative states—individual integrity and autonomy being core values in this work. These asocial conditions support the higher levels of self-commitment critical for accessing the internal landscape of The Self. Instead of depending on external stimuli to motivate self-expression, participants turn within to the body/psyche's innate sources and images to animate their movement.

Asocial Interplay

Paratheatre work offers a window to witness the internal landscape. At some point, a door opens inviting entrance into unknown regions of the body/psyche to experience firsthand the vital forces sustaining our existence, and to give them expression in patterns of movement, vocal creations, and presence. Though the initial training process adheres to the values of solitude and internal dependence, group interaction is explored in *asocial interplay,* but only after participants learn to generate enough personal presence to interact with others from a state of *total offering of the self,* rather than from a place of want or need.

Asocial interplay differs from improvisation as commonly practiced in theatre, dance, and music, where the performer takes cues and energy from other performers in the moment and moves them forward somehow. The difference with asocial interplay is that nobody wants or takes anything from anyone else. Everyone sustains their own state of offering, as a strong force of presence that acts on others, while being acted on by the presence of others in an interaction of mutual offerings. This develops spontaneously in a kind of miraculous interaction of self-governing bodies, where a group unity of sovereign expressions emerges unlike any kind of group interaction I have experienced before or since.

Sacred/Profane

Most of this book documents my personal experiences facilitating and participating in these asocial ritual Labs as written in my journals between 2000–2011. These Labs ran between two to three months each, meeting once or twice a week for three hours each time, and almost always at night. All of them took place in Berkeley California at Wildcat Studio and at Finn Hall where we explored multiple dimensions of **the sacred** but not always the kind of sacred that lends itself to that overly-precious halo effect. Sometimes the sacred turned profane. These allegedly opposing states occasionally interchanged, where the sacred turned profane and the profane turned sacred. This yin-yanging dynamic occurred throughout repeat immersions in our ritual polarity work where we embodied numerous contrary states—such as *weak and strong, safety and danger, pleasure and pain, order and chaos*—that would eventually merge in synthesis, giving expression to their underlying unity. A kind of alchemical union of opposites became an ongoing theme throughout this polarity work which was consistently present in each session of every Lab.

The Gnostic Heretic

I define "gnosis" as any concept-free zone of *direct experience* unfettered by preconceptions, assumptions, and theories imposed by the thinking machine. Though this flies in the face of traditional doctrines of gnosis, it expresses the overarching aim of this Paratheatre medium for restoring the capacity for a more direct experience—*free of societal labels, religious dogmas, and political persuasions.* Though mostly defined by organized religions, *heretics* are seen as rebels who oppose religious dogmas, many of whom were historically persecuted for their confrontational views and positions. A heretic can also be anyone who opposes the *status quo,* consensus reality, and/or any official or popular opinion. A *gnostic heretic* may be anyone who chooses to live in accord with their truths rooted in direct, firsthand experience as their true source of spiritual authority. Count me as a *gnostic heretic.*

Throughout *SACRED RITES,* an alternative definition of **ritual** bypasses the costumed spectacle of robes and wands of Western occult ceremonial magick, the archaic nature worship of pagan rites, and the somber pomp of Catholic High Mass with its tasteless wafers, cheap wine, and sermons chanted in the dead language of Latin. Though these more traditional ritual worlds continue meeting the social and spiritual needs of The Many, they fail to offer the challenges essential to my creative and artistic development. Paratheatre work has acted as an insurrection of the Poetic Imagination for arousing character and story elements in my films, experimental theatre works, and the art life.

When these ritual journals were written, there was never any idea of publishing them as a book. That idea spawned many years later in 2023 after realizing my subjective experiences on this work process might serve others in ways differing from my other books on metaphysical systems and philosophical perspectives. These journal entries never attempted to explain my experiences or pontificate about what they might mean, though I tried to at times. My aim was to simply report what I saw and felt—what I was reacting to—as honestly as I knew how. As a result, some of my entries may seem confounding, irrational, or even absurd. Much of what I experienced had no familiar labels or categories yet. Oftentimes, I had to rethink my process of thinking itself just to find the right words, and often words failed me. Since I also facilitated these Labs while also participating in them, I've included prompts, ritual designs, and the sources suggested to each group I was part of at the time.

SACRED RITES is a sister book to *STATE OF EMERGENCE: Experiments in Group Ritual Dynamics* (The Original Falcon Press; 2020) where the central Parateatre methods, principles, and rituals are codified for immediate application. *SACRED RITES* mirrors the soul of this work, whereas *STATE OF EMERGENCE* represents its muscular rigor and skeletal structures. Working with both books together can bridge the subjective experiences of the internal landscape and the objective external techniques and actions in a more unified vision of what this Parateatre medium is about and what it can actually do.

I also highly recommend keeping a ritual journal if you're doing this work. If you can, write down your experiences without embellishment and simply report what happened. Don't dwell on what it all means. If you can refrain from imposing your analysis and interpretations, the innate meaning of your experiences may have a better chance to rise to conscious awareness more organically. This style of journaling sets up a creative rapport—a dialogue—between Subconscious and the conscious minds—a body/brain loop offering fresh experiences and new ways of seeing.

The Pivotal CRUX Lab

The first offering in *SACRED RITES* is not a ritual journal entry, but an interview I gave on the 1999 CRUX Lab when a group of eight (including myself) met three times a week for five weeks, three to four hours each time, at the Fellowship of Unitarian Universalists in Berkeley over the summer as a "fixed cross" constellation of heavenly bodies hovered in the skies above. Here, we excavated and expressed *the crux* of what each of us were living for through rituals exposing our existential crucifixion, i.e., *where each of us had become righteously stuck*. Brutal, I know. The CRUX Lab was not based in Jesus or Christianity, but a deep dive into the mystery of resurrection through a more universal, non-sectarian crucifixion archetype *made personal*. This CRUX Lab marked a critical turning point that informed some of Lab themes throughout 2011 which is why it's included here (CRUX is documented on video with other Paratheatre videos at: verticalpool.com/paratheatre.html).

The Portland Productions (2016–18)

The final offering in *SACRED RITES* is also not a ritual journal entry but a series of notes and reviews about the five ParaTheatrical ReSearch productions staged at PerformanceWorks NW in Portland Oregon from December 2016 through December 2018. Each production was preceded by a ten-week Lab exploring specific themes and archetypes developed into *living rituals*—spiritual events—disguised as or dressed up as **experimental theatre,** utilizing poetry, live music & song, film projections, theatre lights, and costumes. As a living ritual, none of these "shows" could be rehearsed like the stop/start process common to dance and theatre rehearsals. Each pre-production run-through had to unfold in its entirety from intensive warm-up cycles, polarity work, to whatever sources were innate to the Lab theme *without interruption.* This was also how each production was performed every night and why no night was alike or repeatable.

The Work Continues...

As of this writing, certain individuals I have trained have begun, or may soon begin, leading group Paratheatre Labs. Brazilian native Joao Peixoto in Rio de Janeiro and Jeffrey Fisher in Asheville, North Carolina started initiating Labs over the past several years with plans to continue. In Liverpool, England, Jessica Bockler has facilitated Paratheatre groups. Professional actor James Wagner plans to start Paratheatre Labs for trained actors in New York City. Aikido sensei Nick Walker, who trained with me for ten years in Berkeley, may run his own Labs in the San Francisco Bay Area at some point. Ed "Gensho" Welsh has already initiated several Paratheatre small-group Labs in Portland Oregon and Bryan Smith, in Corvallis OR, tells me he's looking forward to experimenting with groups. Though not trained by me, Mariana Pinzon of Berlin has been leading several hybrid Labs there based on her work in Chaos Magick, combined with methods and rituals from my book, *STATE OF EMERGENCE.*

Whoever explores this work, whether solo or in groups, please know you have my blessings to attempt the impossible, as I have, with as much commitment and autonomy as you can muster. Find your own way and your own style of group facilitation. The vital sources accessed in this work already exist within the Body/Psyche; nothing needs to be made up or created. All that's needed is your agreement to feel your body deeply in the 5-phase warm-up, to embrace an ever-deepening internal receptivity in No-Form, and the courage and self-commitment to discover **a total act of offering of the self…to The Self.**

No-Form→ Dream→ Form→ Dream→ No-Form…

— Antero Alli, March 1st, 2023
Portland, Oregon

"CRUX OF THE MATTER"
Interview
Non-Sectarian Crucifixion Archetypes, 1999

This interview is a response to the "Crux Lab" video document of a private group experiment conducted in the summer of 1999. It was first published in the (now defunct) Seattle WA tabloid, INSTANT PLANET in their November 1999 issue, and also featured in my 2003 Paratheatre workbook, "Towards an Archeology of the Soul". The interviewer is Seattle activist, Jonnie Gilman. — *Antero Alli*

INSTANT PLANET: Did you find with the people participating in the ritual that they had a strong charge to the symbol of the cross in and of itself, and did that get in the way?

ANTERO ALLI: Yes and no. The charge was much stronger for some than others, yet no one escaped its mysterious magnetism. My assumption around the symbol of the cross is that it has deep historical relevance, as well as profound psychological, spiritual, and religious charge—oftentimes deeper than what we're aware of. As a species we've spent the last couple of thousand years in various forms of religious warfare, acting out various opposing and conflicting cruxes of what the cross means. The crux of one culture often differs from the crux of another culture, and when you have conflicting cruxes facing off with each other, the horror of war can be ignited.

I'm using the word "crux" here to symbolize a point of worship, meaning what an individual life or a culture revolves around—what it lives for. Sometimes it can be broken down in personal terms as *"what am I living for?"* If you honestly ask yourself that question, you can begin tracing your responses back to a crux—*a point of worship*—representing what your life actually revolves around—not what you hoped it might revolve around, but what you actually live for.

In this CRUX project, I bypassed intellectual and philosophical discourse on the religious symbolism of the cross. Instead, I presented the cross as a symbol for what the crux might represent to each person without binding it to any historical, religious, or metaphysical context. If these levels came up on their own, then fine. But to fill their minds with past crux references would only impede a more authentic response. I was afraid these past references might overwhelm and interfere with the exposure and expression of something more personal. So, I introduced ritual triggers to this group that provoked, in bits and pieces along the way, elements of what might lead to their most personal crux.

Sacred Rites

The reason for presenting it in bits and pieces was that oftentimes people have a concept of what they're living for, an idea, or even a belief, but when actually confronted with the psychological pressures innate to the reality of what they are living for, those previous concepts often break down. At that point, you either let go of those images or suffer a kind of psychic immobilization, and crucify yourself on a dying concept. And this happened to some extent with everyone. Fortunately, everybody also had numerous opportunities to outgrow their obsolete ideas and restore enough psychological freedom to discover something more innate.

Once you confront the crux as direct knowledge or an impression of a living energy and force within you, it's difficult to deny its existence. Consequently, there is often a kind of ego-death in that confrontation, along with a need to redefine and rethink what you are living for. This crux process may be an ongoing kind of life work. It's not like all of a sudden everybody gets their crux and that's it. *(laughs)* Far more often than not, it involves going through many layers of the crux until you get to something that makes itself evident by the force and the energy it imparts to the life you are actually living. You see, the crux energizes you.

IP: The crux seems to be a symbol of the individual in and of themselves, embodying the horizontal and the vertical that forms the crux. The individual living entity finds himself in the center of these pulling, pushing, equalized forces. They are right there, stuck, pinned to your cross in that way.

AA: In this group experiment we discovered a certain irony to that solitude. By confronting our own individual crux, we saw how we were also connected as a group. We looked around, and saw how we were all nailed to the cross of our own existence. We're all crucified somewhere. Everybody's stuck somewhere. That sense of unity, I think, bonded the group. So, this wasn't a self-isolating ritual. It actually promoted a deeper group unity, but to get to that unity we had to penetrate into our own individual crux first, and that meant arriving at some pretty intense and sometimes painfully lonely places where we were righteously stuck.

You know, there's a fine line between a rut and a groove, and the deeper the rut, the closer the crux. By the way, this whole notion of being deeply stuck or nailed was never presented with any incentive for "self-improvement" or getting "unstuck" as some naive new age idiom. Becoming aware of where you were stuck was seen as a symptom of getting closer to center, closer to the crux of the matter. The overall incentive in this group may've been self-knowledge, and maybe, self-transcendence, but not before some serious and sobering self-confrontations. This was a Reality-Checking Boot Camp.

The word "crux" is a mountaineering term for the most difficult passage on the way to the top of any mountain. This tough passage is called the crux because, if you get through it, you can reach the top of the mountain. If you can't get through the crux, you have to return to base camp, or risk getting stuck in the crux with no promise of rescue.

IP: It's a kind of birth canal.

AA: I relate more to the mountain metaphor. I mean, here was this group on the way up to their own existential peak to discover the edge of whatever they are living for. Each climber had to confront the crux of their most difficult passage to get there, or climb back down to the base camp of their familiar ego-structures.

IP: There is no way to go back to sleep once you have that knowledge. You can't not know that.

Sacred Rites

AA: Yes, it's easy to slip back into sleep. I think that without some kind of ritual device or catalyst or drug or accident to force or shock us back into the heat of our crux, we can nod out again. In this Crux Lab we learned to create our own pressures and ways to keep the heat up to stay awake long enough to always keep one eye open on the peak. Maybe it's an acquired taste for difficulty, a certain excitement for meaningful struggle. Not every struggle or difficulty is meaningful; we humans are woeful adepts at self-torment, and creating meaningless suffering for ourselves and others.

IP: Watching the video, I was struck by the intense analysis that people would go into to try to understand what their motivations were, or what was the heat for them, why they were here, and in some cases, it seemed immobilizing. There's a certain fixed quality to that. In the midst of all these opposing energies and self-conflict, it might be easy to get lost in over-thinking.

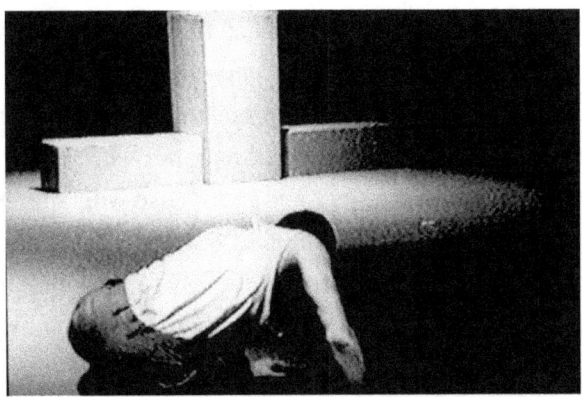

AA: Direct exposure to the crux point can shock the ego. And one common reaction to that shock is this flailing about for answers and grappling for some kind of conceptual understanding. This compulsion to make sense of everything can become obsessive. I think this may be a way the ego naturally attempts to re-stabilize itself after the shock to regain control and make sense of any experience larger than its mental categories. Sometimes ego can tear an experience to tatters while impatiently trying to figure it out. Like a hungry dog attacking a steak, there can be a kind of morbid obsession with creating certitude or control where none exists. This shock to ego involves an exposure to some part of you that unconsciously lives for something other than ego. Ego doesn't want to hear that. What a blow to vanity! Ego wants to believe that IT's what you are living for. Ego wants to believe that IT's the most important thing. And so, the ego will fight back and impose some understanding of what's happening in an attempt to regain its lost ground and territorial imperatives.

Everybody went through some degree of this ego drama. These fixations on explanations came out more in the beginning. The more you go back to the direct experience of the crux, however, the more that experience softens those fixations to try to explain everything. As people were subjecting themselves more to the exposure of their crux, they tended to grow a little easier around that compulsion. There is real mystery in the crucifixion archetype. Over time, I saw more acceptance of that mystery and more ease with simply being in it, rather than needing to understand it. Some showed more die-hard ego-struggles than others by clinging tightly to their dogmas, trying to conform their experience to previous beliefs which only added to their suffering. Sometimes, the crux hurts.

IP: The need for answers is perhaps a form of resistance.

AA: For some, it can be a brutal revelation to be exposed to what you are *actually* living for, as opposed to what you *think* or *hope* you're living for. If you have a negative reaction to what you're living for, it can be like waking up in a nightmare. To live with that knowledge is obviously very challenging. The only creative thing you can do at that point is to show some courage, and muster up some self-compassion to live with more truth about yourself. Sometimes you find out what you are actually living for, and are genuinely excited by that. That's not hell, that's heaven. But if you are waking up to anything you are not ready to live with yet, that may feel like hell, or maybe, purgatory.

IP: Once people grew conscious of what they're living for, and it was distasteful to them, did it compel them to shift that core of what they are living for?

AA: Some would just bury their heads in the ground ostrich-style, and try to escape or deny and pretend they didn't see it. Others would surrender to the fact, and agree to suffer and experience remorse or shame or whatever honest emotional reaction to what they were living for. And I respect that. Maybe they discovered how they had settled for less and felt bad about that. One person discovered that all she was living for was sensation. Her whole life amounted to producing more and more sensation—pleasure or pain, it didn't matter, just as long as more sensation was produced. When she first discovered that, she became depressed. She very much wanted to believe that somewhere deep inside there must be something more to life than just sensations. It was her good fortune that she agreed to suffer through that. She also showed enough courage to bear up to that unbearable truth. By suffering through it, a new vision was born for living for something other than sensation.

IP: The drive for sensation is almost a hunger for perception.

AA: Maybe. But it also could be the result of superficial values. In many ways the CRUX project was about the disclosure of values, of what people were actually making important in their lives. Not what they *thought* they were making important, or *wanted* to make important, or *should be* making important if and when they got their act together. No, it showed them what they were *actually* making important, whether they previously knew it or not. Some people were shocked to realize how dominant the force of habit was in their lives. Others found out how dominant the force of will was in their lives. We're not talking about one of these forces being better than the other, but two living forces that prevail in our lives every single day.

Another important polarity was the more morally charged forces of good and evil, the existing force of good and the existing force of evil. These, of course, are subjective assessments as we're not following any religious dogma or any societal definitions of these terms. I encouraged an openness to the existing conditions of goodness within the group, as well as the existing conditions of evil, as we personally knew and defined those terms. Good and evil were never explicitly defined for anybody. This was no Sunday school lesson...

IP: The jumping off of that crux point to get the perspective to see what I would be living for seems very daunting to me. The cross is so much one's own incarnate self. You surrender to your situation and live consciously with that.

AA: There's a real mystery in the heart of the crucifixion archetype. You have to get over the delusion of self-improvement, and find the courage to commit wholeheartedly to your direct experience of where you are the most stuck, and muster up the courage to continue passing through the very heart of where you are righteously stuck. If you can do this without any fantasy of becoming a better person, or becoming free or enlightened, the mystery of resurrection arises, of being reborn—not just in the Christian sense, but in the mystical sense. There can be an actual transformation of being, and not merely a change of state.

The kind of surrender to *what is* doesn't require dwelling in your problems. It demands 100% integrity in your commitment to following through into the heart of the crux of the human condition, an inner journey that carries no guarantee. There is no concept or image to describe how that will turn out, or what it will look like. It's a genuine mystery in the way that death is a genuine mystery. We don't know what death is until we're there, until it's happening to us, and it still may remain mystery. Same with life; we don't know anything until it's happening. Truth be told, we don't even know what's going to happen next. Uncertainty, like Impermanence, remains an objective truth of existence. Creative artists tend to know the suspense of not knowing what's going to happen next as a creative state. This is how we approached uncertainty, as a creative state.

IP: It seemed that within this group there was a high degree of self-responsibility. People stuck with it, and continued through the process.

AA: Safety was an important factor. In this ritual process, everybody pledged to be responsible for creating their own safety. So, no matter how strange or weird things got, each person basically agreed to play their own mom and dad. With everybody becoming responsible for their own safety needs, it supported a higher degree of personal and group autonomy. Without that high level of self-responsibility, this CRUX lab could never have happened. My incentive in inviting each of these individuals into the Crux Lab was the strong motivation I sensed in them all for increasing their integrity and autonomy.

IP: Yes, I see how safety is very important. When I experienced this work in Seattle, I saw a very risky, almost Pandora's box kind of situation, where there was such opportunity for psychological stuff to bubble up, for projecting mom, dad, authority, or whatever.

AA: Trouble is, psychological projections happen anyway in any group process. It will always happen. The difference is that when you commit yourself to 100% self-accountability right from the start, you can look at those projections as opportunities to begin reclaiming them. In this Paratheatre medium, this unconscious projection process, when made conscious, turns into a ritual skill for evoking archetypical forces and processes when it's done on purpose. The method of *conscious projection* involves intentional charging of the ritual space with a certain energy of your choice. Making the unconscious, conscious continues as a lasting directive in this paratheatrical work.

If you don't do rituals or live life with intention, you may be more prone to passive self-victimization, of feeling overwhelmed by circumstance and self-pity, or end up needing more attention from others than they can offer. This immature behavior leads to feelings of helplessness and betrayal and all the other negative reactions a child acts out when not taken care of and paid attention to. With the intent

Sacred Rites

of self-accountability, you agree to take charge of taking care of and paying attention to the child by monitoring your own behavior and meeting the needs of the frightened child when those fears surface.

IP: In this group-alchemy that happens, is there more of a sense of group mind or group consciousness developing?

AA: Any group unified by some purpose or reason for being there is going to birth a group mind. I was looking to support a very particular kind of group mind based in self accountability, and one that was up for an adventure, a challenge. I tend to look at any novel experience that expands consciousness—whether triggered by ritual or by life itself—as an adventure. My interest in consciousness expansion is not for its own sake; any fool can get high. I look to it as part of a larger development of conscience, something I think is taken for granted in this culture. People assume they have a conscience if they know how to feel guilty. Yet oftentimes this "conscience" is so socially conditioned into us as a life-constricting reflex, it keeps us emotionally locked into a state of ghetto guilt without knowing it. This can manifest as pesky self-consciousness, agitating insecurities, and a stifling of creativity by accentuating the negative in any situation.

If you have not defined your own ethics yet, you've probably inherited your morals from the culture at large and/or your family. Your personal ethos defines in your own terms what you perceive and evaluate as good and what's bad, what's evil and what's right and what's wrong. Experiences that expand your consciousness give you a better chance to see and realize the truths of your life and your own responses, and what they mean to you. When you finally develop your personal responses to these truths, you can define your own ethics and a conscience germane to the truth as you know it, whether it's perceived as right or wrong by the moral judgments of others.

If you are willing to accept the consequences of your decisions and the actions you take, you are free to do as you please with a clear conscience. When you betray your ethics, true guilt stops you to wonder what happened. You can then self-correct, or adjust your ethics. You can apologize and forgive. You are free.

I think this kind of conscience isn't possible without direct experience, the open and honest perception to assess any situation for its good or bad. If you are not experiencing life for yourself, you may have temporarily lost the capacity for direct experience. If you want to restore your capacity for direct experience, you must be willing to struggle and fight for your own consciousness. If you have lost the capacity to think for yourself and come to your own conclusions to determine your truth, then I think you are more at the mercy of circumstance and its backup default programs of consensus—socially sanctioned moralities.

IP: In doing this work, what has been your primary motivation, what compels you to take this on, show this to people, continue it, evolve it.

AA: Personally, I do it to stay honest. If I don't find ways to remind myself of my crux, I slip into cultural trance. I'm not immune to that yet. If I can't occasionally break cultural trance and receive deeper impressions via direct experience, I'm nodding off with the rest of them. I also utilize these labs to break trance so I may develop creative ideas that sometimes bear fruit in my filmmaking and theatre projects. Break trance, create trance...

IP: It was interesting in the Crux video how one gentleman mentioned that it changed his perceptions, his sensate perceptions of the world. Something in the process really does get to essence.

AA: This thing called essence can be a misunderstood term. I know essence as an immutable element of our nature. It doesn't change. It almost has this predetermined, maybe genetic, quality about it, something established at an extremely early age, maybe at one year old, two years old, who knows? But I think it's connected to the crux in that it doesn't change. The closer to the surface you get in your own experiences, with your own self, like the surface of the sea where things noticeably change, the deep core remains quiet within a depth of stillness.

I think as you grow more aware of what is essential to you, it's easier to relate with what is more essential to others. There's also a greater chance of connecting on an essence-to-essence level with others, which I find satisfying. I think part of what the Crux Lab did was engage people at various degrees of essence. When I say various degrees, I mean in proportion to the degree of commitment each person showed to surrendering into the immobilization that sometimes accompanies the crucifixion archetype.

To some people, immobilization meant a kind of death, the worst thing imaginable; the most unbearable thing was being stuck. Others find a little more comfort with this. They find their own place in this immobilization and reach into and through the center of that stuckness. These individuals tend to integrate their crux a little sooner, I think. There are also those who define themselves by motion and change, the slippery characters.

For this Crux Lab, we appointed ourselves nicknames to symbolize our crux. Mine was Antennae. I picked up signals from all the other cruxes and organized them into a video document for transmission. Another person called himself Slippery. This exemplified an important drama around confronting his own escapist habits, and how through more self-honesty he was able to access something less slippery by calling himself on it. One woman called herself Cage to symbolize how her nonstop thinking-machine had caged her into a world she was not happy with.

Another result of this Crux Lab was how it inspired my 2000 film *"Tragos"* about an urban tribe of technopagans performing their ecstatic rites in a virtual reality program that expanded their awareness of what they were living for. Once awakened to this crux, how do we live with more truth about ourselves? Compassion, for ourselves and for others. I have known no other way.

THE RITUAL JOURNALS
Antero Alli, Berkeley CA, 2000–2011

"Orphans of Delirium" 2004, San Francisco

The DREAMING RITUALS Lab
*Choreography with movements
recalled from dreams*
Sundays & Wednesdays, Oct. 15 to Dec. 20, 2000

Lab Intent

To develop a ritual choreography based on movements recalled from our night dreams (see *State of Emergence*, p. 77), and find social integration of these experiences in a weekly dinner at the director's home.

Sunday Nights. DREAMING RITES (Studio). The approach to dreams here is non-interpretive. Rather than pursue any search for meaning and analysis, these rituals were designed and presented to prime the physical/emotional bodies for greater receptivity to the innate essences, forces and purposes within the dreambody/dreamtime itself. The intent: to amplify the overlay between dreamtime and daytime as a portal to initiatic experience and initiation by the Dreamtime.

Wednesday Nights. DREAM COUNCIL (Director's home). The sharing of stories, struggles, and insights unearthed in the rituals and the actual dreams themselves. The dream council provides a forum for languaging the ineffable experiences of dreams and the dreaming ritual itself, towards new ways of thinking and talking about the dreaming.

Participants

Antero Alli, Sylvi Alli, Julian Simeon, Nick Walker, Lea Bender, Brian Jenkins, John Doyle, Cyder Cisk, Oliver Crow, Susan Park.

11/5 Sunday Night Ritual

Every time I check in with dreambody, each experience impresses me so differently it is impossible to form any fixed idea or image about what dreambody is. This consistently confounds my attempts at categorization; whatever dreambody is, it presents itself as a reality beyond my rational mind. Dreambody teases this mind with its autonomy and power; existing beyond the mind, the dreambody laughs out loud and sees through everything.

Humbled by dreambody, I pray to its emanation. My devotion summons subtle forces from within my body, enlivening resonances in me that I give expression to in odd, sonorous chants. It seems that my voice (and song itself?) acts as a conduit for the dreaming, as if the throat were some kind of chamber or vortex the dreaming uses to make itself known; wondrous feeling, to sing the dreaming into being.

One time, the dreambody shows itself as a dark prison with me as prisoner. I pace the cell gasping, wondering why, where is the dreambody I know and love? Why this desolate, utterly despairing impression?! No answers! I am done with this torment and step outside the circle. Returning to NO-FORM, a sudden laughter erupts out of nowhere. Dreambody just made a fool out of me, a big fat dreaming idiot! Turns out, I over-identified with dreambody, and lost all perspective. By becoming this dreambody, I turned into a prisoner of dreams... Another NO-FORM alert. My being is free only when I am not being anything... I need to restore enough space around the dreambody to interact with its emanation.

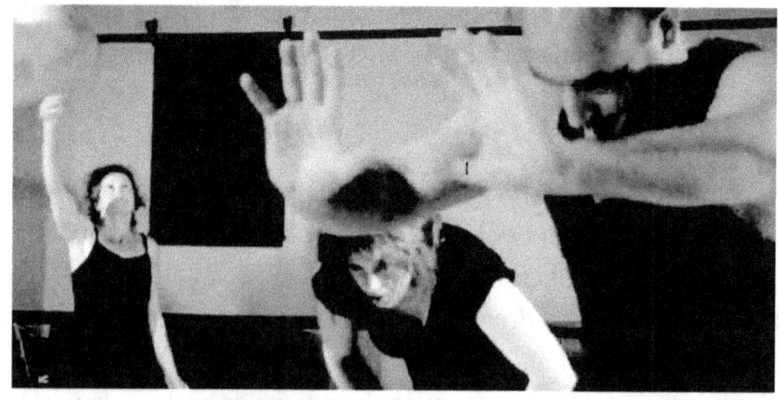

11/8 Wednesday Dream Council

Tonight, we all observed a predominant spirit of resistance within the group (not unanimous, but dominant) especially around dream recall and remembering movements. On closer examination of my own resistance, it soon grew clear that my approach to dreams—going to sleep with the intention of remembering movements—was, perhaps, too direct, maybe even arrogant. Like some midnight stalker of dreams. Who was I fooling? Who am I to determine when and where the dream movement avails itself?

This insight left me in a stupor; a pseudo-scientific idiot with his all-important thesis and experiments. This baggage of excess certainty weighed heavy and rang false. Then, it rang hilarious. I laughed out loud, and shared my embarrassment with the group. I told everybody that my dreambody was a BIG TEASE. This dreambody wants romance, not clinical research and development—the dreambody as dream lover. A revelation. I had to change my behavior to appeal to this dream lover as if I were on a hot date, not some ritual experiment. My previous approach hit a dead end. This is not an experiment, it's a courtship. A romance with a dream-lover called ANIMA.

11/12 Dreaming Ritual

Tonight, the group executed the charged, fluid dreaming ritual for the first time together. Save for a single lit candle in the center of the space, our physical warm-up commenced in darkness, but it was not a silent darkness. This warm-up cycle conjured up its own cacophony of howls, screeches, yelps, and cries. A chorus of chaos, a jungle night swarming with hungry ghosts and dreaming spirits. Was the group animal afraid? If so, no fear was spared in giving ourselves over to expressing it all vocally. Then again, maybe I was the only one afraid. I was tired, exhausted, and a bit intimidated by memories of past dreaming rituals and their sudden, penetrating effects. I let go of these memories. I had only enough energy to surrender, and I was not going to piss my power away on mind games.

After the warm-up, while the others jogged around the setting's periphery, I went to each of the four corners, and lit a candle. Now there were five lights—the outer four illuminating the periphery, and a single light marking center: the dreaming zone. We stood in No-Form outside this designated "zone of the dreaming" with the intention of entering it open, and letting the dreaming have its way with us. Under the influence of the dreaming, we began our 3-part movement cycles to establish and maintain a personal reference in this dreaming zone. I encourage the group to exit the dreaming zone, and reconnect with No-Form whenever necessary; we all moved in and out of the dreaming zone for about an hour.

 I enter the dreaming. Everything slows down, turning malleable, plastic. Before losing myself to the dreaming, I initiate my first movement. The moth; I inhabit the moth. The posture forms tightly, and fills with the dreaming, my voice now a conduit for the buzzing of my new blue-dusted wings. I hover, suspended in this buzzing when the second movement emerges, as if from the buzzing itself, and now I am standing playing this musical instrument only I can play, a strange melody plucking my vocal cords, notes warbling out not quite right as the third movement emerges, an angry reaction to this warping music. I stand there and grunt; the sound of this grunting holds me, or my perception of me, together. This 3-part movement cycle continues its permutations and breakdowns. I could do this all night long. Something in me collapses, I fall to the floor and crawl out of the dreaming zone, back to No-Form.

 Standing in No-Form. I walk zombie-like around the periphery of dreaming zone before slipping back inside it again, surrendering to the ongoing permutations of my ritual choreography now being shaped by the dreaming until its structure and the dream become one and the same. Now everything is easy—the movement, the sounds, the transitions. Everything is so easy it scares me, and this fear I am now feeling is a signal. Something important is happening. This fear is a signal. It is time to leave the dreaming, return to No-Form, and end the ritual. I do. I return to No-Form.

11/15 Dream Council

Nine of ten dreamers are present; Julian is absent. Tonight, everyone shared the dream circumstances around each of their three movements (selected for their dreaming ritual movement cycle). It turns out that everybody's movements originated in separate dreams. As a result, we all listened to remnants of twenty-seven dreams. I admit to suffering bouts of boredom listening to the dreams of others, but this was different. I was transfixed. Each movement, and its accompanying dream context, expressed qualities that were poignantly germane to each person. The group as a whole also showed degrees of genuine interest: intrigue, fascination, awe, amusement, horror. No analysis or search for meaning was expressed or encouraged. Disclosure of the dream circumstances around each movement seemed enough.

As the night progressed, another common awareness surfaced. We all expressed recognition of at least two levels of dreaming: 1) dreams that seemed chiefly self-referential and 2) dreams of visitation from or communication with a presence of Other; i.e., not self. The first dreaming contained obvious projections of one's personal psychology, family gestalts, and/or psychic regurgitations of the day's stresses, frustrations, and fantasies. These dreams seemed to serve the processing of familiar impressions. The second dreaming engaged encounters and confrontations with genuinely unfamiliar, alien, and/or autonomous entities, beings, and realms or dimensions. That we all are aware of this distinction, these two dreamings excite me. I express similarities between this second level dreaming with my personal encounter with ayahuasca, an Amazonian vision brew. Both act on my consciousness as vivid initiations with Other. Both impress me deeply with a sense of real communication; i.e., no mere mental chatter or projection often confused with, what to me is, real communication.

11/26 and 12/3 Two Ritual Nights

Under the weather with fluwhatever I notice two different types of attention. In my brain fog, my attention is heavily anchored in the most mundane concerns: drinking fluids, blowing the nose, eating, and many other bodily secretions unfit for print. No dream-recall whatsoever; fluwhatever needs more sleep than dreams. But what's odd is how this attention seems aware of the existence of another attention. What I can discern is that attention #2 is firmly anchored in non-mundane strata of experience which includes the realm of dreams. It also feels as if this second attention functions autonomously, on its own time. Before now, I was convinced my ability to pay attention was entirely volitional, and made up of one process expressing various degrees of will, effort, and concentration. Not anymore. There are two distinct attentions, a mirroring, like twins in the womb with simultaneous feeding cycles nurturing separate but related growths. Though I don't understand the importance or meaning of this, it exists nevertheless.

12/3 Second Dreaming Ritual

This group took four weeks to complete the first dreaming ritual cycle. This second ritual cycle comes together in half that time; after two weeks, everyone has three new movements from new dreams. The setting: a single lantern anchors the center of this dark temple, throwing cavernous shadows onto the walls and ceiling. We enter the prayer circle (yes, we have been praying to the dreaming for several weeks) with a question or a need. Soon, a cacophony of sounds and chants erupts from this circle of prostrating dreamers. We rise and roam as shadows, and at some point, gather together in a small No-Form circle, a formless sanctuary; standing there with our backs to the lantern, we face the outer shadow regions that are now dedicated to the dreaming. My only instruction to the group was to take more time by allowing the dreaming influence to have its way with you first before applying the physical movement cycle.

All three of my movements are from the same dream and this dream takes place in a mansion inhabited by powerful, yet benevolent spirits. All three movements also happen to be movements I perform every day in my mundane life: 1) walking, 2) opening a door and walking through the doorway, and 3) punching in a phone number on a touchtone telephone. From No-Form, we all step forth into the dreaming zone. I fall forward and the shadows dancing on the walls suddenly remind me of something and then, I'm there.

Walking the floors of this mansion. The other dreamers appear as shadows passing me by in these massive corridors under cathedral ceilings, chandeliers, wallpaper designs I've never seen before because they are designing themselves. Gentle winds gust, and I am in a hurry to hide somewhere, not knowing why or if someone is after me or not. A door appears to my right and I open it. One of the mansion spirits lives inside this chamber. I am unafraid but respectful, that respect for unknowable powers. I turn around, look across the hall and see an armed guard staring me down while punching a number into his cellphone. In a flash, I become this guard. I'm punching this number into my cellphone while talking to myself across the hall, "I know where you are now."

My three dream movements continue in various permutations, each one turning into a living symbol that the dreaming is using to send me a personal message. I can decipher this message whenever I am walking, passing through a doorway, or punching in a phone number. I just have to exercise enough dream recall to notice and remember myself when I'm doing these things, whether that's in the dreamtime, or in my daily mundane world; memory is everything.

Closure; the End? (A Surprising Truth or Two)

Within the timeframe of this group lab, we underwent three separate dreaming ritual cycles (of 3 movements each), with each one differing from the rest. In retrospect, I admit to being surprised that we actually pulled it off, and now I am a little saddened by its ending. This crew of dreamers created an oasis, a sanctuary, amidst the workaday world and its hypermedia non-culture. We found refuge together in our active prayers to the dreaming, and in rituals built from movements originating in our dreams.

The richness and complexity of this experience was such that nobody expressed any need or desire to impose meanings or cosmic philosophical rants; to be moved by the dreaming was enough. The dreaming is enough. Our receptivity was rewarded by the highly personalized, secret messages the dreaming sent each of us through those gestures and movements we faithfully enacted. To our credit, these personalized messages remained (mostly) secret, thanks to very little psychotherapeutic show & tell. Most of the words we did express came as stories, the telling of what happened in the experience of the dreaming, and in other instances, the personal night dreams of our source material.

What began in my mind as a strictly asocial and chiefly vertically-oriented ritual intent, was subverted by the wilder blossoming of an unexpectedly novel social event. Splendor! Delight! Wednesday Night Dream Council began with the delectable grope of a blind date; nobody knew what to say or the right way to say it. Between tremors and silences, a language erupted. A way of speaking rooted in the sensibilities now aroused by whatever we were experiencing in the Sunday Night labs. Dream Council nights sparked the telling of related stories about ghosts, the human aura, scary archetypes, personal violation, the differences between men and women, control vs. power, and the occasional reference to childhood traumas to be expected with any sincere pursuit of truth.

Dream Council also provided what I had hoped for: an anchor to integrate our Sunday Night rituals. This anchor infused a deepening sense of safety, trust, and faith critical to maintaining receptivity to the dreaming, the archetypal force shaping the more genuinely strange and miraculous states of being I could ever, and could not ever, imagine.

The ANIMA/ANIMUS Lab, Spring 2001
7 Sundays, 3/18–4/29, Wildcat Studio, Berkeley

Anima/Animus Lab Intent

After enacting my solo ANIMA SHRINE rituals over the years, I decided to expand the format for group application. We are six women and six men. Each of the other eleven participants in this Lab were chosen on a hunch that every participant was already in an active struggle, conscious and/or unconscious, with one or both of these archetypes. I ascertained that they all showed enough ego-resilience to endure and benefit from working with these emotionally-charged archetypes.

I will facilitate the rituals and participate in them. It's time for a personal reality check around the current conditions of my own relations, and lack thereof, with the Anima. I've been noticing changes in her appearance, and some possible new functions she serves. I need more insights only ritual exposure can offer to her sources, as well as my own.

The ritual plan is to start simple by developing a gender-specific relation—*men to Anima and women to Animus*—until we all feel ready to experiment otherwise; i.e., switch archetypes (it's my assumption that each anima expresses a kind of meta-animus and *vice versa*). The following ANIMA Lab Journal entries are my attempts to report the subjective and psychic impressions these rituals evoked during my processes of contacting, courting, embodying, extracting myself from and renewing relations with the Anima...

Participants

Antero Alli, Sylvi Alli, Nick Walker, Christa Ray, Brian Jenkins, Heather Hanan, John Doyle, Jonnie Gilman, Diarmid Baillie, Serene Zloof, Seamus Qin, Jane De Cuir.

4/1 The Anima Ritual

First impressions of the existing conditions of the anima surface—after the physical warm-up in my private temple space—as a playful S&M cage scenario, but without the cage; the collar around my neck is attached to a very long, silver leash (astral umbilical?) held by her, somewhere beyond sight, yet definitely above. This leash doubles as a communication line. I have the distinct feeling that without this line, I'd be lost. Truth is, I am still lost on the collar yet connected; I hear her laughing, "Better lost with a collar than lost without." I agree; this anima feels compassionate. This basic feeling of attachment soothes the slave; welling emotions...happy slave/sad slave...one and the same.

I ask Anima for a vision. A very young and very blonde maiden appears in a small rose garden. An elevated, porcelain birdbath in the center overflows with water, rose petals, and splashing sparrows. Watching the birds, I slowly walk counter-clockwise around the birdbath, my left hand trailing in the cool water, fingers grazing feathered wings, drifting petals; I am the maiden. I sing my song of innocence. Nothing self-conscious or perverse, but rather a lucid dream of genuine serenity, the simplest of joys. In this moment, nothing exists beyond the garden. I thank anima and return to No-Form outside the temple.

Immersion/extraction, a group polarization ritual; immersion in the Anima/Animus, extraction from the Anima/Animus. Time definitely slows down in the immersion area; spatial awareness expands in the extraction zone. These impressions are heightened by a sense of freedom in extraction, and of being bound in immersion. After physically moving between these two areas a few times, I notice a crossover synthesis. I earn some autonomy in immersion (picture a slave with attitude), and a clarity of form in my movements through extraction, a quasi-martial arts choreography of swift angles and windmill slices; the slave also dances.

Final ritual: distillation of immersion; everyone stands in a large circle, facing center where, on the floor, there is a large cross. This cross area is designated to extreme immersion where we are to crystallize that essence into full-body gesture. Inside this gesture-crystal, we react to those around us (who are all executing the same directions). When done, we step backwards, extracting ourselves with every step from that crystal of immersion until reaching the No-Form zone at the circle's periphery. Everyone underwent three cycles of this immersion/extraction ritual, producing three vivid "crystals" each. Emotion oozes through my gestures, my reactions to being anima's dog; my melodrama of anguish, protest and howling at the moon.

4/8 Full Moon Yesterday, Still Full Today

First entrance into personal temple. Standing in No-Form, a dimming memory appears: it's me as anima's dog. I am so over that. I let it go, drop down into No-Form, and enter the temple. Looking around, I see painted walls; a tent-like yurt. The scent of musk. I look up, and there above me quivers a giant luminous vulva, pulsating between two swaying legs. Laughing out loud, I am a lusty satyr trapped under the hoop skirt of a very large and sexually aroused Anima. I sit down, inhaling the musk; I'm delirious, exhaling like some cheery drunken Jack Nicholson with horns, a goatman-god crazed with too much of a good thing, eyes rolling back up into my head; self-intoxicated, ridiculous...

Rising on my hoofs I begin dancing in spirals, as anima legs wrap around my neck, the glory of the moment enflaming a terrible vision: I am the goatman. A bolt of fear jolts my goatman body, my fate. The inevitable sacrifice of the goatman-god to the Goddess, the scapegoat martyr: *Tragos!* I turn to the Anima and confess, "I know what this is. I'm ready to move on, I want to evolve." I am suddenly impaled by a very long spear. Struck down, falling, I am dying. Very slowly. Dying, and then, I die some more. This goes on until the old satyr is finally dead. I exit the temple, and return to No-Form.

After a group polarization ritual exposing the negative and the positive anima, we all enter a large, collective circle devoted to the conjunction of negative and positive anima/animus energies. This volatile mix seethes with molting patterns of motion. I serve these patterns, giving expression to their shifting rhythms, their erupting choreographies twisting my body this way and that. Unpredictable, mercurial, liquid fire. This totally exhausts me, yet I need one final return to my personal temple to check in with the anima dynamic. I share this direction with the group, and we disperse to our separate temple spaces.

Upon entering mine, I am surprised by the calm. The Anima hoop skirt is gone, replaced by what appears to be a vertical cone made of spun glass—milky, silky and smooth. Standing inside this cone, I am awed by its purity of unified energy; no divisions or cracks. As I stand there, my body begins rotating clockwise. In this turning, I perform a strange yet familiar ritual, as if in my sleep. What is this? I can't put my finger on it, but keep doing it anyway. I know what this is. Benediction. I am a priest in the temple of a goddess performing a ritual benediction. Anima as deity. My priestly function: to honor Her presence. And the more I do this, the more aware I am of Her emanations, blessed gentleness, permeating everything with subtle luminosity. Very peaceful. I could stay here all night, but instead I exit the temple and return to No-Form.

4/15 Half Moon

After entering the personal temple space, I sense an absence of "Anima charge," and step back outside to deepen my No-Form. As No-Form deepens, I ask the Anima to "show me what I need," and then step back into temple space. Anima is gone, yet her answer to my question is everywhere: I need risk. My emotional need for challenge is seriously frustrated. Shit. I actually need awareness of danger to feel alive. My body turns clockwise, a slo-mo whirling, my mind flooded with images of an emotional plague immobilizing individuals and society with its deadly apathy, unclaimed guilt and anxiety. This is danger enough.

The toxic shock of so much backed up, unexpressed, repressed responses to life experiences. The Great Unwashed. The Bottomless Tub of Runny Shit. Corrosive Emotional Slush. Don't identify with it, I repeat to myself. Dis-identify; don't be it, relate with it. The emotional plague, a horrific nightmare of species ignorance. I don't like being this sensitive to the shit tragedy of the world. It's too much. I feel sick, and then, just as suddenly, I hear her whisper: "Just deal with your own shit." Anima; what a gal. I thank her and return to No-Form.

A group ritual; a large circle designated to the "potency" of Anima and Animus. At the outer periphery of this large circle, everybody stands in No-Form facing the center. The ritual intent is metamorphic, or multi-phase: 1) step in and absorb the potency of anima or animus; 2) let the absorption increase until you embody the anima or animus; 3) let this embodiment own and possess you; 4) when you feel the need to liberate yourself, extract or release the anima or animus from yourself, out of your body; 5) relate to it as an autonomous energy that takes form outside and beyond your body; 6) communicate this relationship in a dance; 7) after the dance, say goodbye to the anima/animus, exit the circle and return to No-Form. My personal experience in this ritual holds too much value to write it down.

In the final ritual, the group space is divided in two—men on one side, women on the other. Each gender group owns their collective space. From there, the men move towards the Anima zone, and the women towards the Animus zone; the intent: to embody Anima/Animus as a character. On the men's side, we whoop it up; hooting and hollering like there's no tomorrow. Vainglorious noise; just like men. When we're done, we stand there dumbfounded, No-Form rolling over us like fog on a battlefield. Shoulder to shoulder, somnambulist soldiers inching towards Animaville. We're inside now within her numen. My knees buckle, tremble; my body splays open, skeletal scaffolding collapsing in on itself.

On my back and vulnerable, the Anima sends me Irene: fiercely devotional, a nun, singing wordless holy songs through my gaping mouth. Singing to the Holy Virgin Mary, clutching my rosaries, I rock back and forth, my soul rising and delivering to Mary, and delivered by pious sexless devotion. A rosy-white heat swirls in my brain. Sweat oozing down my face, I rise to my knees and move about singing, spreading emanations of good will, mercy, and kindness. Blessings from Mary through Irene through me throughout the space around me, when a small yet distinctly male voice calls to me. That's funny; I can't understand a word he's saying. I follow an impulse to return to the male area, where my manhood suddenly redeems itself. Happy to be back, to be a man, to be in No-Form.

4/22 New Moon Approaching

There we were, shoulder to shoulder, all twelve of us standing in No-Form. Behind us, the legacy of anima/animus (all we've been impressed with in this lab and beyond), and in front, what remains unknown about anima/animus. My body tilts ever so slightly back, and then forth; touching past, touching future, until I'm sucked backwards into a vortex. The air is dense, textured, multi-layers of accumulations of past Anima projections and heartbreaks. The air here is so...thick, like treading water, as if water were muck'n'mire. I feel myself sinking deeper into, and supported by, this strange mud-like inertia. I see two choices: continue sinking and drown, OR walk on the mire like it's ground. I walk; I walk around on what feels like compacted layers of emotional sediment. I walk around humming this little dixieland ditty, and then return to No-Form. Standing in No-Form, I'm thinking how easy that walking on the mire felt; maybe too easy? No; not this time. Easy does it.

4/29 Final Lab Session

The first twenty minutes of this final lab, the group defines a single temple space with twelve altars—six to the Anima, six to the Animus. Walking past each altar, I notice artwork, stones, feathers, a dozen roses and even more oranges, photographs, a naked doll, a disconnected computer keyboard, a dog-eared copy of my 1987 book, *All Rites Reversed,* a quartz rock, and other fetishes too unrecognizable for words.

The night ends peacefully with dignified closure for the group as a whole. Several profound and subtle impressions. The freedom disclosed in an Anima-free zone, a place where no Anima exists (designated as the area outside the temple); pure revelation. Also, an insight into a new context for the Anima in my life: her presence appears as pointless (and stupid) around interpersonal relations, as it is meaningful (and smart) around creative research. Not Anima as muse, but Anima as guide or scout; the Beatrice/Dante connection. What strikes me as important now is not the Anima herself, but the relating with her, and the finding of my autonomy in the Anima-free zones.

I am at peace with the Anima. Don't know how long this calm will last; I know how tempestuous she can be. Yet a new understanding does surface between us tonight. This shared vision holds too much value to articulate and spill, and so it remains our secret. I'll discover, in time, what I'm learning—if anything—by what I'm actually able to apply in the course of daily life. Until then, I know nothing.

I step forward into the unknown Anima, and my right hand rises slowly over my head. There she is, above and before me. Guiding me. Beatrice. Like some kind of Dante, I am led by this Beatrice in such odd ways around the space, around the others. These are small moves. We take tiny turns here and there, turns I never would've thought of

Sacred Rites

taking on my own. They feel meaningful and inconsequential, deep & meaningless. The sense here is that anima guides me to recesses of the unknown (unconscious) I could never discover otherwise. Her guidance also feels dangerous yet extremely valuable, like dangerous art. She shows me how no art comes from the conscious mind; if it does, it's dead art. She shows no conscience for my peace of mind; it's up to me to limit our time together. If it were up to her, she'd continue jerking me around like some plaything. She has no respect for my mind; she only wants my body, to possess it. Who can blame her? A lot of entities would die to inhabit a body, and some do.

The final ritual: a gossamer vision of midnight faeries. After an extensive embodiment and extraction process, we all develop separate dances with our now extracted and very autonomous anima or animus. The air is full of spirits. There are now twenty-four of us; twelve people dancing with twelve spirits, each dance distinct from the rest, yet unified by everyone dancing with spirits; a midnight ballroom of waltzing faeries. These dances interact with each other in lyrical will-o'-the-wisp fluidity. I drift beyond the circle, happy; my face streaming with sweat as everything returns to No-Form.

The ANCESTORS' Lab—Autumn 2001
10/14–12/11; Wildcat Studio, Berkeley
Sunday Night Dinners & Tuesday Night Rituals

Lab Intent

We entered the Ancestors' Lab a month after the 9/11 terrorist attacks in New York City amidst the shockwaves rippling across this nation and the world. I chose this theme, maybe naively, as an appeal to *ancestral wisdom* for potential healing and insight during this new, highly unstable era. However, I couldn't completely romanticize my ancestors—or the ancestors of others—as consistently wiser men and women who never made catastrophic decisions leading to epic fails. After all, they were human, just like me and my friends. Yet we heard their call, and this Lab was our response.

The first phase of this Lab aimed at engaging the forces and pressures innate to parental conditioning. Our aim was to identify them as behavioral patterns, and then explore the options of either accepting them or revolting against them. I felt this difficult, yet relevant, self-work with *family karma* might empower a more honest approach to the deep wellsprings of earlier ancestral memories with their hand-me-down, clan-defining customs, stories, traumas, and codes for assuring future survival. Through full-on commitment to experiencing personal family dramas as a basis to launch into the impersonal collective ancestral archetype. This Lab also inspired elements in my 2001 film, *"Hysteria",* exposing the racial profiling threatening many Middle Eastern families in the USA following the 9/11 attacks.

Participants

Antero Alli, Sylvi Alli, Nick Walker, Heather Hanan, Kyra Auerbach, Lea Bender, Lissa Ivy, Jonathan Furst, Jane De Cuir, Tom Evanoff.

Sunday 14 October—Orientation Gathering

Orientation gathering and dinner. The participants shared their reasons for being in this lab, or why they thought they were there. Though our motives varied, all seemed united by a common thread of respect for the influence family has had, and continues to have, in our lives. We spoke about ancestral lands that shaped its culture, and the diverse geomantic properties of the bio-regions we were raised in.

Jonathan F. talked of growing up in the Arizona deserts, with its wild pigs, snakes, scorpions, killer heat waves, and water scarcity. We learned of Sylvi's small town upbringing in "backwards Mississippi" (her words): the humidity, the daily sameness. Then, there was my own early life in the winter blizzard lands of Helsinki (Finland) and Toronto, before eventually migrating further southwest to virtually weatherless Los Angeles. Several others told of being raised around heavy urban sectors (Trenton NJ; Pittsburgh PA), dense suburban tracts (San Fernando Valley), and rural farmlands (Sonoma County). Then, there were quasi-nomadic stories of being moved around a lot as kids. We hail from diverse climates and topographies, all of which continue living in us—in our cells, our memories, and our emotions. I suggested that everyone start collecting artifacts, letters, and photos from their families, and store them in an "ancestors' box" that we'd dip into throughout this lab.

Tuesday 16 October—Ritual night

Though I was participating in most of the warm-up, I chose to remain outside the ritual tonight for an overview of this group, and to monitor the commitment levels in the all-important physical warm-up (which went very well). After the warm-up cycles and some peripheral jogging accessing the earth's energy—the Earth Jog—I suggested the group polarity of Mother/Father as the existing conditions of M/F and all that belongs to M/F. The group engaged this polarity with little to no resistance, their hunger for these essences now obviously satisfied.

After a second-wind warm-up cycle, the space was drawn and quartered for the next ritual: a quaternary of Mother, Father, Child, and Ancestors (with Mother opposing Father, and Child opposing Ancestors). The Ancestors' area was left vague and undefined to respect that mystery. Once this second ritual was underway, I suggested a shift of focus from "reacting" to these forces to "serving" them—i.e., of serving their expression rather than just reacting to them. This shift, from reacting to serving, proved revelatory to some participants who later in the ending group circle voiced their epiphanies. This fourfold ritual structure felt potent enough to merit future use in this

Lab. Tonight, both rituals were illuminated by a single candle flickering inside a lantern at the center of the space. My overview assessment of this group is that we are ready to do this Lab. We are ready to enter the Ancestral dimensions.

Sunday 21 October—Dinner gathering

Tonight, there is less socializing and everyone seems to eat their food either faster, or they just eat less; I can't tell. I show *"FEARS"*, a short film I recently completed using Rilke's poem, *FEARS*. This opens up a Pandora's box of childhood fear-stories in the group; some fears were actually thrills, not fears *per se,* while others expressed sheer childhood horror.

I share my early fear of old men who owned property. I recall this old man in the house on the hill surrounded by a labyrinth of bushes that my friends and I wandered around in. This old man would walk down the hill into this maze, and shake his big stick at us, shouting swear words; this was always a big thrill as we scampered down the hill like frightened rabbits. After telling our stories, we placed several relics from our Ancestors' boxes into the center of the room where I had lit a candle. We then prostrated ourselves in prayer around our makeshift altar, and prayed to the ancestors to see what would happen.

Several of us report strong impressions of unity with ancestral images and energies—cellular, biological, genetic. I experienced two distinct levels in my prayer of the human and the impersonal. I am impressed by this undying sense that ancestors are human beings with insecurities, fears, weaknesses, and strengths just like me—not mythologized phantoms. A sobering revelation; embarrassing in that good way. The other impression delivered a powerful felt-sense of my physical body as a single, yet connected link in a chain of bodies that had lived and died before me.

What I have assumed to be "my life" turns out to be sustained by biological processes existing for centuries before I was born; a humbling, empowering knowledge. One person protested, saying that she only prayed to God. I find this assumption at odds with my belief that people and God are indivisible. Fascinating; I would not have been aware of this belief (as a belief) without her dissent. Different scenes for different genes...

Tuesday 23 October—Ritual Night

I began my full engagement as participant. As everyone arrived and found their transition into ritual space, I lit a candle near the east wall, and designated that area as an altar for the group's ancestor relics; a collective altar. I turned all the lights off. We all stood in No-Form with our backs to the west wall, facing the darkened ritual space (designated as "the Ancestors' space"), and began our gradual approach to the group Ancestral altar. Here, my prayers somehow summoned the word "perseverance," a word that took on new meaning as a facet of my ancestral code. As a Finn, I knew winters could be very hard in Finland; if you do not persevere, you don't survive. Something pristine about this spirit of perseverance; crystalline, almost. I felt like I had to let go of whatever I was unable to persevere.

After the physical warm-up, everyone prepared their warm-up areas as "private temples" for their personal polarity of Mother/Father. The Mother-space oozed a drippy martyrdom, while my Father-space burst out with fierce fighting movements. Both were extreme, pure, and abstract, and completely at odds with each other. After exhausting their separate agendas—*the martyr sobbing herself dry, the fighter collapsing*—they eventually fell into each other's arms. Ain't love grand? Next up was a group polarity: Whatever Is Family/Whatever Is Not Family. Another piece of the code emerges for me in the Family side: "We take pride in loving our children and this is how we persevere." This experience restores my faith in basic goodness.

Soon, I rediscover a new aspect of my family identity. After venturing over to the "Not Family" side, I become enraptured by an ever-expanding consciousness incited by my life beyond the gene pool. *I am a frontier scout of my gene pool,* exploring the outer limits of what had never been experienced by previous family members, with the exception of my frontier-scout mother who initiated our long southwestern migration from Finland to Toronto in 1956, and then to Los Angeles in 1962.

Sunday 28 October—Dinner Gathering

Standard Time resumes (clocks set back), and the group staggers in at differing stages. By the time we're all here, there's such a rolling cacophony of party chaos that I almost forget this is a Lab, and I start drinking too much Merlot. I realize this after muttering something to Jane D. about never having prayed while drunk before. Needless to say, nobody prayed, at least not formally. Instead, I ask everyone what they've discovered over our two ritual Lab nights as a chief obstacle or resistance (I sensed frustration surfacing in the group). After listening carefully to each story, I offered specific suggestions to engage their resistance as energy, as a resource to be tapped and expressed. Given the specificity of my feedback, I am curious to know if it will be applied in Tuesday's ritual Lab. Doubts emerge. Sometimes specific directions can be effective; other times, they're too defined.

Tuesday 30 October — Ritual Night

After the group enters No-Form, we all step into the candle-flickering Ancestors' space. Stopped in my tracks, and unable to absorb anything...nothing happens. As I yield to inaction, an impulse arises to move throughout the workspace for the Ancestors, and not just for me alone. As I continue responding to the space as I move, my energy escalates. As this intensity gathers momentum, I direct its force into service to the Ancestors.

What develops in me is a sense of protectiveness (my own or the Ancestors? I don't know), and then I find myself stalking the outer periphery of the room, its borders, like a sentry guarding a fortress or a treasure, like that was my job. As long as the borders were secured, my purpose was fulfilled. This guardianship ritual marks my transition into the warm-up and my personal polarity of Grandfather/Grandmother. Here, I discover and imbibe the gentle emanations of mercy (grandma), and the electrical jolts of severity (grandpa) that expand in me and give rise to the Stoic (grandpa) and the Saint (grandma) who eventually crystallize as two statues facing each other on a garden floor of dead leaves.

After the personal polarities, we all convene in the No-Form corridor for the group polarity of Parental Conditioning/Innate Being (who we were before impacted by parental conditioning). Much of this complex experience proves too large or too valuable for words. What I can say is this: parental conditioning acts on my innate being as a structuring force critical for the manifestation of my dreams in the out-there world; a kind of boot camp training for the earth-bound soul.

I discovered something about my sense of humor. If I was able to stay connected with innate nature while moving throughout the parental conditioning, I could laugh off the family guilt trips and the strictness of rules. It was extremely funny doing everything I was told. Laughing while totally obedient. How weird is that? On the side of innate being, the experience confirmed a profound inner strength and an innocence born from wisdom, not naive ignorance. Both sides of this dynamic polarity were clearly in cahoots with each other, serving a larger purpose of preparing and testing the incarnating soul for planetary life. This polarity proved profound for others, as well. I was pleased to hear my Sunday night suggestions were applied to good results. I feel the empowering results of this ritual will stay with me as long as I can stay in touch with my innate being and with my sense of humor.

Sunday 4 November — Dinner Gathering

Everyone but Heather H. arrives (she phoned in while driving back from her daughter's wedding). Within minutes, it seems, we're all sitting in a circle chowing down with nary a word. After dinner, I ask if anyone's relation to their ancestors or family has changed or picked up since the lab started. A snowballing momentum of family stories rolls throughout the circle, save for Tom E., who remains pensively silent. My story. Between my mother working two jobs to assure our survival, and my merciful grandmother cooking all our meals, my childhood was enriched by a deep faith in a silent sense of invisible benevolence. With mom's absence and grandma's discreet cleaning and cooking, an unseen—yet always felt—spirit of basic goodness pervaded our home. Deep down I also knew that even though my mother was not around much, the results of her absence gave me and my brother the freedom to wander and explore life beyond the nest, having too much fun playing in the streets with neighborhood kids to feel anxious over not knowing where my mom was.

Tuesday 6 November — Ritual Night

Standing in No-Form, with our backs to the Ancestors' area, we gradually step backwards into it, and I am struck by an immediate sense of *strangeness*. All previous memories of unity or sympathy with ancestors dissolve. In its place there's a distinct feeling of not belonging. I did not want to be there, yet there was no escape—no exit from a place I didn't want to inhabit. Very uncomfortable. I paced around the periphery, and then tried to pose as someone who "belongs" there; I even stood in a corner thinking nobody saw me. I became aware of the omnipresent Ancestors watching me. Very uncomfortable.

I take solace at my personal Ancestors' altar, and see the photograph of my (now dead) father smiling, holding baby Antero. I bend down to pray, sending him my apology for being a deserter from the Finnish army (a true story, too involved to tell here). Feeling his albeit reluctant forgiveness, I rise from this prayer, and re-enter the Ancestors' Space. The strangeness disappeared. Nobody is watching me anymore. I suddenly feel like "one of the crew," and walk about with arms outstretched, embracing the space before me. A sense of grace and peace surrounds and pervades the space. Unity restored and atonement realized. I had only to feel my dead father's forgiveness.

Sunday 11 November—Dinner Gathering

Happy Birthday, Antero. Tom E. brings party hats and silent tweeters; a chain reaction of birthday wishes domino towards me. I'm 49 today; seven sevens, half a century minus a year; the final year of my forties. This year, this number 49 feels dramatic. As it has turned out so far, every ten years my life has passed through an initiatic portal. Migrating to the USA from Canada at 10; starting over on my own in the San Francisco Bay Area at 20; starting over on my own in Boulder, Colorado at 30; starting over at 40 after the death of my second daughter, Zoe. Is there a pattern here? Will life start over, still again, at 50? If so, is there anything I can do to prepare?

I ask everyone how family conditioning and Ancestors has, or has not, picked up steam in their everyday lives since this Lab began. The usually quiet Nick W. speaks at length of a renewed and deepening communication with both his mother and father, as well as how family values now inform his decision-making processes more than before. His experience brings him a greater sense of internal stability.

I tell Nick and the group how my awareness of family/ancestors amplifies a state of free-floating anxiety. I knew my immediate family as a continual dissolving into groundlessness and uncertainty, which I responded to with anxiety. Yet I find myself now relating with this same anxiety more poetically, as if it were a creative state. Though uncertainty breeds anxiety, it can also express flexibility and openness to change. These days, I am transforming my 9/11 anxiety into writing a screenplay about characters with differing reactions to the heightened uncertainty in this post-9/11 era in my next movie, *"Hysteria"*.

I ask the group to share examples of how their rebellion happened, or didn't happen, while living at home with their families. Their stories were personal and forthright. Their candor conveys to me a readiness for more *individuation* in the Tuesday night ritual work, which means distinguishing oneself from the guilt complexes and the tribal rules innate to early family life and ancestral memory. Now is the time to rediscover one's own voice, one's own vision amidst the clamor of the clan. Seems like this group is ready for more individual integrity and autonomy around family and Ancestral karma.

Tuesday 13 November—Ritual Night

First ritual. The entire floor of the workspace is designated to the Ancestors, and its center—illuminated by five candles forming a diamond shape (N, W, S, E, and Center)—to the "infinite ancestral hub." From No-Form, I step into the larger surrounding area, and am impressed by how vertically charged everything is. I sense an unending chain of religious Lutheran rites of devotion linking generations of Finns. I am now walking around inside a very large church. I cautiously enter the Ancestral diamond hub, when suddenly all these Christian images combust, and I am free-falling inside a Sami/Mongolian shaman wormhole. Fierce animal images, spirits and demons flash before my eyes; a Tuva hunting chant spontaneously erupts in my throat. I sustain its power briefly before exiting the hub. The surrounding outside area feels tame in comparison, yet still related to the volatile inner sanctum. I return to No-Form.

Second ritual. We all stand in No-Form around the periphery of the space, now designated as "family/ancestral soup," the personal and the impersonal, combined. The center diamond area is assigned the source of "the Diamond Self," devoted to essence of original nature, distinguishing us from family identity as individuals, unique in ourselves. Surrendering to the Ancestral group, I feel spineless and owned by this ancestral family soup. Helpless and too passive to change anything, I watch my body gyrate in a mechanical dance bouncing me about like some crazy wind-up toy. As if by accident, I slip into the diamond area and the mechanical apparatus suddenly breaks down.

A strong lucidity surfaces, enveloping me in deep calm. On re-entering the soup, I notice how safe I feel within this diamond self. I recreate my role there from my own diamond integrity. This new freedom and power feels almost too good to be true, and I start doubting it. However, it is not the Diamond Self that doubts its power and freedom. It's family guilt. Family guilt doubts anything threatening its control, as it must. Then I, as the Diamond Self, laughs off the bogus family guilt, and returns to interact with the Ancestral presence; family guilt was never my guilt to start with.

Third ritual. The entire space is re-designated as "the Diamond Self" (the candlelit altar area is where "offering to Ancestors" can occur if we wish). From No-Form, I step into Diamond Self and absorb its shock. I am crushed by its immense freedom, and crumble to the floor. Going by the previous ritual, this is not what I expected. On the floor, I responded to this shock by serving–giving expression to–this freedom. At first, through very small movements that gradually develop their own ecstatic momentum. Soon, I am upright and dancing like a banshee, writhing and wriggling throughout the space, my entire body a spasm of joy erupting in perpetual self-discovery. After exhausting my physical energy, I approach the Ancestors' altar, offer up my thanks, and then return to explore new ways to engage this Diamond Self in movements, gestures, resonating sounds, and overtones of joyous noise.

Sunday 18 November—Dinner Gathering.

We listen to stories and recollections of family dramas and ancestor-based issues that many of us have been confronting daily since last Tuesday night's ritual lab. I think that perhaps the exposure and immersion of that "diamond self" ritual may have brought to surface-consciousness certain underlying conflicts, such as forces of oppression or family guilt complexes threatened by the emergent autonomy of self.

Sacred Rites

The group was growing more aware of specific parental conditionings they were entrenched in, or were mechanically acting out in Victim scenarios. Many expressed genuine difficulty in facing these internal dramas. I suggest that a certain type of difficulty could mean something important is happening, especially if it demands facing conditions that are now unavoidable, inescapable, and undeniable. I think this difficulty gains significance as it forces us to confront self-denial and escapism, buffers to self-acceptance, and transformation. This "bearing up to existence" builds an internal strength, not based on ego, but in the will to exist, the will to be. I ask everyone to identify their role in their drama, to find a personal polarity that somehow connects to this role, and then to bring this to Tuesday night ritual. Jonathan F., confused, asks: "How can I know this role?" I tell him his role will probably develop from his relationship with the drama, not the trauma itself, and how he responds to it. I couldn't tell if he got what I was saying.

Tuesday 20 November — Ritual Night

A dramatic ritual night. After the physical warm-up and personal polarities, we all gather in the center of the space—shoulder-to-shoulder—standing in No-Form, facing the central lantern before our feet. At the outer periphery of the workspace, four candles flicker. To the north, the Father altar; to the south, the Mother altar; to the east, the Child altar; and in the West, the altar of the Ancestors. Gradually we step backward into No-Form, unfurling our way throughout this temple, passing into the field of each altar, stopping to worship or grieve or sing or simply sit. At the Ancestors, I rage like an animal; I'm pissed off and don't know why, but it feels good. I find serenity at Mother and thank her for this piece. At the Father, I find myself singing a wordless tribute to Arto, my dad. Over at the Child, I am clapping my hands, jumping up and down and laughing. In pathways between the altars, I was floating along on No-Form's gentle cloud of Unknowing.

The second ritual uses the same structure as before, the four ancestral archetypes. Except for one big difference. Everything beyond No-Form is broken—Broken Father, Broken Mother, Broken Child and Broken Ancestors. The only unbroken area is No-Form. This ritual truly flipped our expectations. After being swirled around in the No-Form area like some cosmic swizzle stick, I eventually visit all four corners, and offer my body over to each as a sacrifice, giving expression to the unique brokenness of each. Movements, emotions, sounds, gestures I had never known pass through me like so much oozing crackling splintering light substance. I heard sounds of wailing, raging and laughing all around me. The others were reacting to their own broken realities by finding ways to allow these forces to pass through them, their voices, their souls. I started realizing that it's a back-and-forth thing, this reacting to the brokenness, and allowing its expression through us. There's more here but words fail me.

Sunday 25 November—Dinner Gathering

Tonight starts out typically with most everyone in the kitchen talking, eating, and then reconvening in the living room. Very soon thereafter, I don't know when or how, we all slip on this cosmic Marx Brothers banana peel, and raucous hilarity breaks out. Sylvi, the laughing perpetrator, cracks us up with her appallingly funny "evil pixie" routine. We're in stitches. Then, there's Jane D.'s big fish stories, and my own ridiculous pantomime antics. Outrageous, cathartic, entertaining, we were obviously ready to blow off some steam.

After our little laugh-riot, the group energy descends into an extended lull. I even suggest that maybe we're done, and that everyone should go home. No reply. I ask everyone if they've noticed any significant changes in their dreams lately. Almost everyone reports increased dream activity which compels me to ask the group to bring a dream movement to ritual on Tuesday night. Then, Tom E. stirs things up by sharing a resentment with Sylvi's antics and her mentioning Jonathan F.'s really loud and persistent burping during Tuesday night rituals. Tom E. thinks Sylvi and I are ganging up on Jonathan F., and then wonders what the rules are. I tell Tom E. that I don't care if Jonathan F. burps. Sylvi expresses her disgust, calling the burps "crass" and "not sacred." I say the only real rule in this ritual work is developing integrity as individuals, and through that, respecting the integrity of others. How this occurs, however, differs for each of us. Sometimes conflicts can trigger delayed reactions that prove more beneficial than their initial annoyance.

Tuesday 27 November — Ritual Night

We set up an area dedicated to the "Ancestors of the Ancestors"—big, expanded family-tree kind of stuff. As I step into this zone, I am startled by the immediacy of my embodiment in this source. No time to respond or relate with anything. Instantaneous manifestation, like water quickly turning to ice. The upper vertical area of the ritual space looms large with the presence of entities, and soon the entire room becomes like an amphitheater of disembodied souls long departed, at home as the dead. I am a piece of this; there's no difference. This piece that was me walked about with a super-charged, physical stiffness, like open-eyed sleep paralysis. I passed by the photos and relics of my Ancestors' altar. These objects, and those they symbolize, felt like descendants, children of the older souls now watching us. A different perspective. Ancestors, like me, are also children of Ancestors.

Back in No-Form, again, facing the ritual space now divided in half: the first half designated as Dream; the second half, the ground—or Earth—of the Ancestors. Passing into the Dream, I collapse to the floor, and gradually begin rising through layers of dreamstuff as the songs of whales reverberate throughout my internal body cavities; stomach, diaphragm, lungs, throat, mouth, nose, and brain. I step over into the ground of the Ancestors and instantly (again! this immediacy) incarnate as this hot-blooded, Sami warrior full of piss & vinegar. I'm stomping about, clapping my hands, hooting and howling like some damn fool possessed by devic sprites of the aurora borealis. Possessed by a terrible, murdering glee!

Sunday 2 December — Dinner Gathering

Tonight, I sensed a major turning point in my own relation with this lab. I confess to the group that I entered a dark night of the soul, a nadir point, in this Lab. I know this place. The familiar "dark night" symptoms were all there: low energy, confusion, disorientation, depression waiting in the wings. All the family-based immersion processes, my own emotions around that, have resulted in an over-saturation of family burden, a feeling of over-ripeness gone rotten, gone to seed. I suggest that maybe it's time for me to stop so much processing, and start distilling these raw impressions through more clarity of form; less sauce, more meat, please.

Along with this need to distill came this sense that the group might be ripe for an increase of asocial interplay in the ritual space; more articulation, less emoting. Fortunately, these perceptions are soon confirmed by the group. Unanimously. We are, indeed, ready to distill these essences and approach asocial group interplay.

Tuesday 4 December—Ritual Night (final entry)

"Heart of the Ancestors" ritual. Tonight we witnessed a major fruition ritual, born from the fecundity of all our previous immersion processes. My experience, impressions, and expressions were so vivid, ineffable, and numinous, it feels pointless to write about or attempt description. Instead, here's the ritual structure itself.

First, we eliminated our personal Ancestors' altars; no photos, relics, icons, or family object fetishes. The temple space feels more clean, free of spirits; the only entities here feel like the Lab participants. After the physical warm-up, the room is divided in half by a No-Form corridor: "personal heart" on one side, and "heart of the Ancestors" on the other side. After enough immersion in both, we return to No-Form, and then jog around the workspace to create a transition, and then return to the No-Form corridor. The same Heart polarity–Personal and Ancestral–but this time, we enter with the intention of finding movements and sounds that best serve the Heart of whatever realm we are in. We also allow interactions with each other through these movements and sounds. This goes on for a while, and then we return to No-Form.

After another transition jog, we all take new No-Form positions at the outer periphery of the workspace, now as temple. From No-Form, the direction is to step into Personal heart, and walk a spiral path of the Personal heart (counter-clockwise) towards the center of the space which is designated as Ancestors' heart. At some undetermined point along this spiral path to the center, the Personal heart merges with the Ancestral heart. We agree to resonate sounds as we each enter this merging point. A procession unfolds, a rotating spiral of Heart paths, aural cacophonies, and vocal formations develop, erupt, encompass the group. The Ancestors arrived to greet our miraculous interaction of self-governing bodies, choreographed by the Personal Heart. We have distinguished ourselves as individuals in the company of the Ancestors.

Throughout this final night, I started receiving images of ancestors beyond my gene pool, images of women dressed in what appeared as Middle-Eastern attire, perhaps from Iraq or Iran. This looked like two sisters arguing about something, maybe their family. This struck me as a possible lead to a film idea percolating in me about the 9/11 attacks where I wanted the terrorist to be a fundamentalist Catholic, not an Islamic jihadist. I decided the sisters would live next door to him. That was it. This became the dramatic set up for my 2002 feature movie, *"Hysteria"*.

The HOLY TRINITY Lab—Autumn 2002
The Sustaining Power of Core Values

Lab Intent

To experiment with multiple sets of personally charged trinities towards discovering a core, or "holy" trinity *(State of Emergence,* p. 83), representing the three most essential sources currently infusing strong value in our daily lives—as in what makes our lives worth living. Though no religious associations with this Holy Trinity idea were presented, they did arise for some of us. Everyone was responsible for naming their own values, sources, and trinities within the given ritual structures provided. Personal autonomy guided the group as did the self-work of facing potentially difficult sensations and emotions around not knowing what made our lives worth living.

4 September—Setting It Up

The "trinity" theme was set apart from other Lab themes by its enigmatic emptiness. In marked contrast to the previous Ancestors' Lab, the vital sources we were tracking were not readily apparent until well into this Lab. To prepare the ground, the preliminary warm-up cycles incorporated personal trinities, rather than the customary personal polarity. It took some getting used to, but soon our minds started thinking in sets of three. Trinities. We also explored several tried-but-true group trinity rituals (head/heart/gut, savior/persecutor/victim, etc.) to develop familiarity and resonance with the triad source structure itself. This was done in the faith that the triangular design might attract something more personal—maybe more essential—to each individual as their Holy Trinity.

Throughout the first eight sessions (the first half of this lab), four of the thirteen participants dropped out. After this, the pace and focus accelerate. About two-thirds of the way through (by the 12th session), many of us are discovering core trinities that lead us into our Holy Trinity. For each Lab session, a three-cornered ritual floor plan, covering the entire workspace, is marked by candles and designated as the Trinity Temple—each corner has an altar with a candle. The nine remaining participants simultaneously superimpose their own personal trinities onto these three altars within this Trinity Temple. We all worked our core trinities collectively, each altar charged with nine different energies. We designated the "pathways" connecting all three altars as No-Form corridors—allowing enough receptivity to be influenced by whatever altar we were approaching next.

In these No-Form pathways I discovered specific relationships among each of the three altars, how each one acts on and influences the other in distinctly personal ways. Moving through two rounds the temple, a possible core trinity emerged:

The Body—personal energy, my own space; my psychology
The Ancestors—ancestral karma; unknown family legacies
The Muse—impersonal spirits of creation; visionary nature

Walking in No-form from the Body altar, I approach the Ancestors' altar with dread and respect. On arriving at that altar, I am surprised by the enveloping sense of support there. I also notice a slight loss of my integrity, and brush it off as a temporary symptom of trading my freedom for clan security within the familial bond. On the pathway from the Ancestors, I walk in No-Form towards the Muse. I sense the Ancestors I've just left behind viewing me as a hero by leaving their safe fold to enter the dark woods of the Muse archetype where witches and sorcerers work their magic. The Ancestors want me to retrieve some new kind of power there and bring it back to them.

A sense of foreboding and sacrifice haunt my entry into the Muse altar realm. When I arrive, my allegiances rapidly shift away from family, and towards the gods. I laugh out loud; am I mad or is this genius? I am dancing like nobody is watching. Sweating, I leave the Muses, and embark on the No-Form pathway returning to the Body. In the Body, I feel a bemused detachment here. Have I become some phantom entity returning to my own Body? A strange sensation to be on the outside of the Body looking in; an out-of-body moment, but not an out-of-mind state. I feel intact. As I slip back into the Body, I kneel in prayer to the Earth, to my Body as the Earth. Earthbody. Faint sounds of wolf howling sing through me.

10 September

I enter the trinity temple as if all three altars are expressions of one physical body. The Ancestors become the *prima materia* of DNA-produced physicality; all personal distinction dissolves into one orgiastic, unified organism. A pleasantly sinking inertia has me drifting down through heavily-textured layers upon layers, down and down into this velvet-black singularity, this ancestral gravity well.

With great effort, I lumber away from the Ancestors towards my Body. Entering my body, I am spontaneously distinguishing myself—my body twitching with delight, temporarily liberated from Ancestors' gorgeous oppression. I start No-Form walking from the Body towards the Muse, slowly astonished by its Otherness. Upon entering, I discover that the distinction gained in my body allows me to open up to, and be touched by, life forces beyond my body; energies beyond DNA-ancestry yet, somehow inclusive of them. Subatomic quantum states? Whatever it is, I experience true mysticism here, an open-ended union with life within and also beyond my body, beyond Ancestors, beyond the Muse...beyond...

The INITIATIONS Lab
Winter 2003 to Spring 2004; 11/30/03–3/20/04
3 nights a week, 4 months, Wildcat Studio, Berkeley
ORPHANS OF DELIRIUM performances March 13–21

Lab Intent

To experience and give form to charged initiatic states. *Initiation* was approached as a mystery. Participants were left to discover, define, and test their own ideas and definitions of what true initiation meant for them. The overall ritual focus was with *heightened physicality, verticality intoxication, vocal creations, and dream ritual choreography (State of Emergence,* p. 67). Everyone vowed to be fully self-accountable for their safety, their creative states, and setting their own pace, boundaries, and limits. I facilitated this Lab about 75% of the time, and participated within the group the rest of the time.

Though it was not planned from the start, this Initiations Lab culminated in the public performance vehicle of *"Orphans of Delirium"* using Samuel Coleridge's opium dream poem, "Kubla Khan", which was spoken by one of three performers embodying the Head, Heart, and Gut of an Actor on an absinthe binge; the Head spoke no other words but this poem. All performances were filmed and made into a video document (paratheatrical.com/delirium.html).

Participants

Paradox Pollack, Serene Zloof, Alaska Yamada, Brian Livingston, Nick Walker, Julian Simeon, Desmonde Daisy, Gabriel Dietz, Adam Palermo, Justin Palermo, Zoe Alowan, Jakob Bokulich.

12/21/03

On the seventh session, the quaternary of the Four Elements (and aether) was introduced as the first major group interaction ritual in this INITIATIONS Lab. I was grateful to have waited. As a whole, individuals expressed a strong show of commitment to serving their own sources before and during asocial interplay with others, which redeemed the ritual from turning into "soup," bogged down from excessive merging of energies or social considerations. Instead, the group energy demonstrated a combustive power to evolve, die, and be reborn several times over; a real delight to witness such a beautiful vision. The previous three-week focus on asocial values, such as No-Form, Spatial Awareness, Verticality, and Source Relations, paid off.

12/23/03

Tonight the focus shifted from asocial interplay to solitary exploration of the internal landscapes. The chief sources were *God of the*

Head, God of the Heart, and God of the Gut. The group as a whole showed as much commitment to surrendering to these internal sources as they had shown to interaction last Sunday. This would not be happening if the overall commitment to No-Form were also not deepening, which it seems to be. True to the spirit of Winter Solstice, an uncommon depth and stillness pervaded tonight's final ritual of Deity Approaches. Participants were more vocal in the final group circle, expressing their fears, excitements, and questions with a candor unseen before this point. I reminded the group of the initiatory phase we were in, of gaining access to the internal landscape and its sources. How it looks right now is not as important as establishing a stronger commitment to serving the sources themselves. We are not looking for a "look" yet, but more emotional honesty and autonomy; the "look," I said, would emerge later on its own.

12/28 & 12/30, 2003. Two Sessions

12/28. Tonight's session started in a group circle where everyone shared their name and why they were there. The group went on to earn more autonomy by undergoing the first 70 minutes of the session without any external verbal cues from me. As a result, I got to join in the Praying Circle, the Physical Warm-Up cycles, and Personal Polarizations (love/fear). The rest of the night was spent exploring a trinity of human systems as sources—1) Central Nervous System, 2) Skeletal, and 3) Muscular systems—first as the movement vocabulary exercise, and then as a group interaction ritual. In the final group circle, I offered each person specific attention points or directions to experiment with in the following sessions. Everyone seemed to appreciate the feedback. Several breakthroughs were made known by Justin, Alaska, Brian and Serene.

12/30. Tonight, a new level of group unity was realized through an in-depth exploration of the trinity of Creator, Destroyer, and Nourisher. The group came to this unity by virtue of each individual staying true to their own vertical source (one of the trinity), while interacting with each other, and being acted on by others. As a result, the group spirit underwent many cycles of transformation, rather than suddenly peaking out and dispersing. Theatrical elements emerged—*near-mythic forms and recognizable motifs*—from the primordial chaos on the floor.

I felt the group was strong enough for more challenging directions (like Shadow work), and expressed as much in the final group circle. I also raised the technical point of people dwelling too long in a given source with the resulting self-indulgence. I said it was up to each person to find that "point of too much dwelling" on their own. I joined in the first 90 minutes (personal polarity: art/life), thus continuing my shift from facilitation to participation.

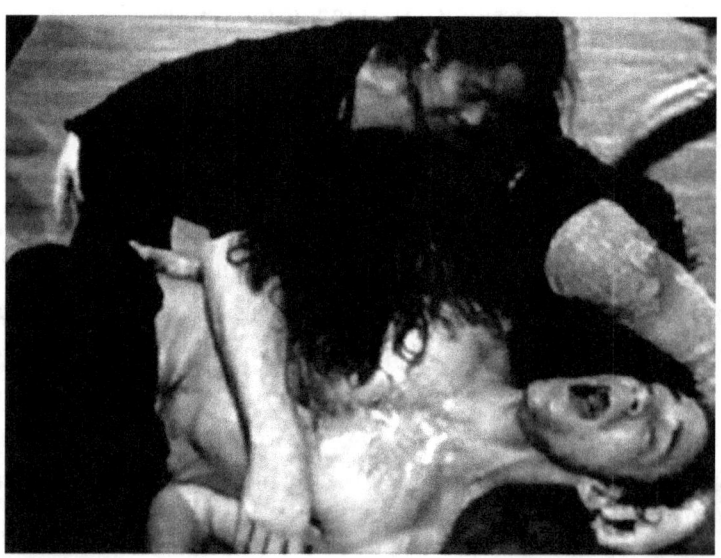

Sacred Rites

12/30–1/02/04. Seeds of a Future Mythos...

1/02/04. In the last lab session, I witnessed more mythic elements spontaneously erupting from the primordial chaos of the group rituals, leaving me with a series of vivid impressions. Since that night, certain seed ideas have started to form in my consciousness involving a specific theatrical framework—a mythos—to contain and present the naked rituals of paratheatrical process as performance. I will await further fermentation before disclosing them to the group. Until then, I am impressed by the commitment and faith this group has shown through their passage into *terra incognito*.

1/04/04. Altering the Expected...

Tonight's session unfolded with surprising results and several breakthroughs, while being the first time I participated in all the rituals (while verbally positing the occasional notes). My personal polarity (disease/healing) served the expression of a bad cold I was just getting over; the results were revelatory and exquisite. The group entered a strong ritual-circle design evoking dynamic polarities of safety/danger and sobriety/intoxication. We witnessed what Paradox later called "some crazy shit" in the center area where individual forces of danger and intoxication mixed and mingled in combustive displays. Though not entirely No-Form induced, the ritual did act as an important release valve for underlying pressures innate to this male dominant group. The overall effect seemed to be one of creative imbalance, a tilting of the group animal towards the discovery of new responses in a well-timed bump into initiation.

1/06/04. No-Form Adjustments

Right from the start, I alerted the group to a few adjustments in the No-Form process to experiment with more potent sources. This included me ringing the gong at random (and not so random) intervals throughout the night as a self-remembering device. *"When you hear the gong, check in to see if you are forcing or controlling the experience, or letting an actual source move you."*

The group then underwent a series of immersions in the Persecutor/Savior/Victim (or Martyr) trinity, resulting in a slew of surprises and breakthroughs for just about everyone. In the final group circle, I announced that I was going ahead with the post-Lab performance level, and that more details would be forthcoming. Samuel Taylor Coleridge's "Kubla Khan" was mentioned as possible text with *divine intoxication* as the context for the rituals. I also reminded the group that Sylvi would be joining us to act on the ritual environment with her soundscape—tones and music amplifying the energies sourced onstage. I sensed we were at a turning point that would articulate itself in the final four lab sessions.

The Final Four Nights

1/11/04. Full house tonight; 14 with me & Sylvi. I opted out of the warm-up, returned to silent witness mode where I introduced the Head, Heart, and Gut as sources to inform three kinds of movement. I can tell the group unity had deepened since there were far fewer collisions out there on the floor. Seems like the group has discovered how to swarm together rather than bump into each other. Sylvi and I huddled in a far dark corner playing a variety of instruments to influence the terrain of the complex Reincarnations rituals. The floor was divided into four consecutive eras across the entire workspace—*Being Born, Living & Maturing, Dying & Death,* and *Afterlife or Bardo*—and then return to Being Born to repeat the cycle manifesting a new life each time around. After the group underwent several reincarnations, they finally exhausted themselves. I settled on "Orphans of

Delirium" as the title for the performance-ritual production we will transition into after this Lab.

1/13/04. Everyone is present except Brian L. No outside music was played. Throughout this session, we explored the vocalizations as a resonating chamber for the sources to sound themselves through us. The group passed through the Head, Heart, and Gut centers, finding tones innate to each source. I suggested the focus of "not forcing the sound," but relaxing the voice, allowing the source itself to do the work. This eventually allowed the sounds to emerge with greater subtlety, power, tonal, and textural variation. The Four Elements were re-introduced next as sources with distinct tones, as the vocal creations continued. This ritual encouraged a broadening of the overall group vocal range and depth. In the final group circle, discussion was stimulated around the formation of language from sounds originating in nonverbal, silent sources.

1/18/04. Everyone is present. A return to initiating the session with spatial awareness instilling the Praying Ground ritual with new vigor and focus. It seems that active relation to space consistently reinforces the asocial climate opening to Verticality. A 3-part vocal process was then introduced—*source to movement to sound*—as the group moved through Head, Heart, & Gut centers. We went through two cycles—once to open it up, and again to distill the expressions. The rest of this session engaged the group polarity of Core Self & Superficial Self. The ritual structure was a large spiral encompassing the entire workspace floor, from the periphery of the Superficial Self to the Core Self center. This rite culminated in a new depth and group unity through a delightful choral cacophony that seemed to satisfy a new collective need for more felt unity. A pleasant silence fell upon us all in the final circle.

Sacred Rites

1/20/04. Everyone is present. Most of this final Lab night commenced in darkness illuminated by a single candle-lantern lit in the center of the space, projecting dancing shadows against the walls. The archetype of Dreaming pervaded all the rituals. The closing rite involved projecting the dreambody into the darkened space, and entering with the intention of looking for it. If we found it, we were to embody it, and let this develop into a character with sounds, words, and gestures. I did not participate, but witnessed in awe the dance of light and shadow, the poetics unravelling before me, the playful fluidity, mystery, and lyrical power of it all.

I shared my vision of the characters and overall structure for the next stage of our journey, of preparing ourselves for "Orphans of Delirium". To cross this bridge from self-initiation to performance, I suggested replacing the word "lab" with the word "vehicle." The lab was over. Our new objective was to build a vehicle to transport us from private ritual time into public performance space. Looking back now, I see how this INITIATIONS Lab was successful in achieving its intentions of realizing individual and group levels of initiatic experience. I am left with feelings of gratitude for everyone who made it happen. Then we took a ten-day break before returning to the performance vehicle (that was also made into a video document).

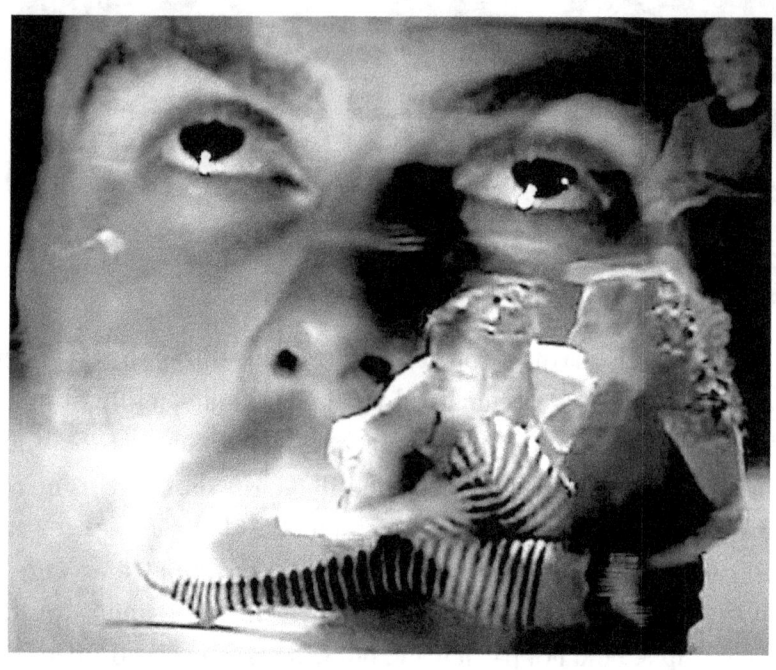

TWO-FACED CLOWNS Lab—Fall 2005
Sundays & Mondays, Sep. 18–Dec.19
Sourcing Hypocrisy as the Personal Clown

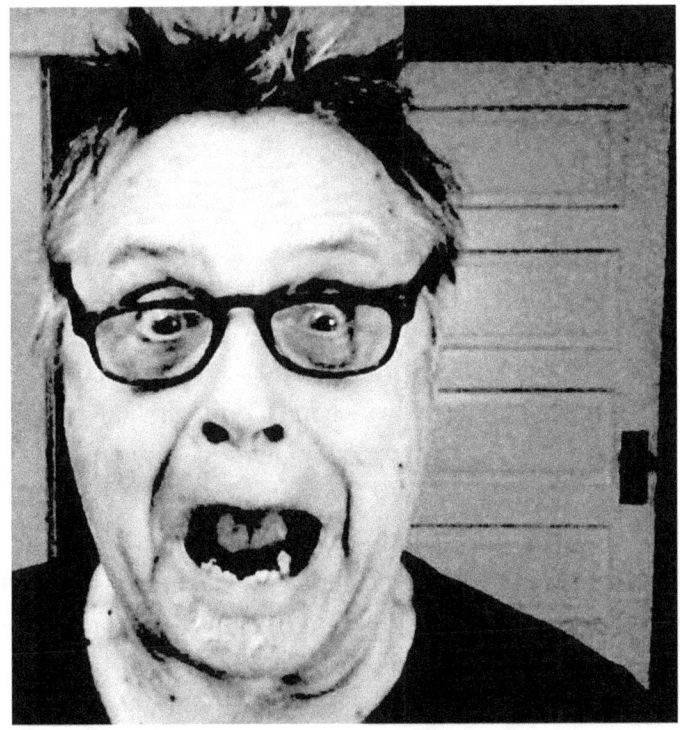

Lab Intent Interrupted

What began as a creative process of exposing and expressing our personal hypocrisies as "clown characterizations," did not culminate as planned in "Two-Faced Clowns", our anticipated ritual clown performance production. Exposing our personal hypocrisies as these often-hilarious clown characters led to painful traumas and a greater need for healing these open wounds, rather than place them on display and trounce about in a sadhappysad clown masquerade for all to see.

Participants

Antero Alli, Robin Coomer, Nick Walker, Jojo Razor, Brendan Random, Matthew Purdon, Wendy Vastine, Paradox Pollack, Brian Livingston, Kate Gibson, Linda Rose.

November 25

From the very start of this Clown Lab, I brought up the necessity to increase self-compassion during our journey through the difficult psychological terrain of exposing our two-faced egos and their hypocritical behaviors for our clown characters. Everybody agreed that this was a good idea, and that we'd give it our best shot.

During the first trimester (9/18–10/17, 2005) of this 3-month Lab, this group demonstrated a robust self-expression around the characterizations of personal hypocrisies in duets and trios of clown-like performances. During this period, I saw how invigorated we were by the shock of freedom afforded by exposing these hidden aspects of ourselves, and shamelessly and hilariously assaulting each other with our exaggerated antics of animated self-importance and other two-faced egotistical monstrosities.

This freedom was catalyzed by a sanctification of "true" and "false" selves as equal in value, blurring their borders, and allowing a more flexible ego in the creative process. Also, I had introduced characters to each participant based in my intuitive impressions of what was already developing in their presentations—characters that proved engaging to them all, and helped clarify our relationships with the other clowns. All in all, the first month's work saw an exciting process of opening ourselves up to ourselves and each other in new and unexpected ways.

The first two weeks of the second trimester (10/23–11/6) saw various stages of withdrawal, from a scattering of absent participants, to a lull in the sharing of stories and observations during the final group circle. In this closing circle, the group energy felt muted, as if the previously more dynamic "opening" phase either frightened us or forced us inward to process what was exposed and displayed so flagrantly to others. It appeared to me that the group as a whole was unable or unwilling to raise their self-compassion during this critical integration stage. The increasing absenteeism was not helping the group morale, and we were also rapidly outgrowing the characters I had selected for us. Something was happening; I just couldn't tell what it was yet.

During the final two weeks of the second trimester (11/7–11/20) the group had completely lost its way. We were clearly flailing. We were severed from the original ritual intent of "exposing and performing our personal hypocrisies." I could no longer see any purpose to what we were doing, and told the group this. These two weeks were difficult for me, as I really wanted to perform our ritual clown show, but I also realized we were facing specific limitations which I chose to respect. Moving into any performance "just to perform" could never work. We needed another intent, another reason to move forward as a collective.

During the first night of the third trimester (11/21), the previous ritual intent of "exposing our personal hypocrisies" collapsed and gave way to a new intent. Things were getting too personal, and our bruised egos needed a break. It was time to shift towards more transpersonal sources such as "dreambody" and "earth surrender." This new transpersonal direction went over well with the group. Like a species of savannah beasts silently drinking from the same watering holes, a new depth and calm enveloped everyone now.

December 6

At this point two participants, Linda R. and Matthew P., withdrew for reasons of their own, leaving the remaining nine as the consolidated core of this post-clown lab. At this point, I invited Paradox Pollack back into the lab (he withdrew earlier to work with me on his solo performance project). With these changes, the lab direction took on a decidedly deeper, more spiritual tone. This occurred through accessing the sources of Masculine/Feminine and their dynamic merging, and the "Deity Approaches" where each of us designated the opposite side of the workspace to the presence of Higher Self, Holy Guardian Angel, or Divinity. Each physical approach across the space to this Deity-presence compelled an honest relationship with that presence. We approached and entered this Deity presence three times: once to find out what it is, the second pass with a question, and the third time with an offering of some kind.

The results of these rituals effectively renewed the group unity around the intent of receptivity to vertical source work, rather than the original intent of displaying our cracked ego-structures in public performance. With every night we were moving deeper into verticality, and further away from the more horizontal, audience-based experiences. In retrospect, I see how the rituals during the end of this Lab foreshadowed the upcoming Spring 2006 Alchemy lab.

The Final Group Circle

The group circles that convene at the end of each night's Lab session have become more telling of a deepening group unity as we shared stories and charged ritual moments. This in itself was extraordinary since usually these participants were quiet, silently processing their experiences, not wanting to verbalize anything almost out of some primitive shyness, as if their hot and holy states might vanish if they talk.

I reminded the group that it was important for the left-brain languaging processes to catch up with their right-brain intuitive impressions, and that the group circle was an opportunity to hone those skills. You don't have to explain anything to talk about it. If you just confess what happened and leave it at that, nothing sacred disappears. You may have even developed new codes and speech patterns for more truthfully reflecting the mysteries experienced. I also announced my absence for the next lab session where Nick W. will take over time-keeping responsibilities, and act as the group's third eye for that one night. This lab continues for six more sessions. On the 17th we decide whether or not to invite witnesses in for our final night, Monday December 19th. The unknown beckons...

December 13

After what could have been the two most powerful sessions of this 3-month lab, the group unanimously decided against presenting any public presentation of what we had been developing. The work now felt too valuable, too naked, too deep to share with an impersonal public coming to watch and judge us, or expecting to be entertained. Monday night's closing group circle lasted 90 minutes (the longest ever) due to the spontaneous emergence of everybody's stories, charged moments, and revelations after the last Reincarnations ritual (exploring No-Form, Birth, Living, Death, Afterlife continuum).

Since the lab intent shifted around 11/22, the quality of each session's work significantly deepened the authenticity of self-expression and vertically-aligned interactions. Every session's results kept getting deeper and more intense than the last. This will be my final journal entry of this Lab. Most of what I experienced over the last two nights has been impossible to put into words.

December 19

Postscript. On Saturday, 12/17, we reinstated the Deity Approaches ritual that achieved a deepening of group unity. Sunday, 12/18, we worked with personal trinities to activate new source relations for us that provided a foundation for our next group extensive immersion in the Creator-Destroyer-Nourisher Temple ritual. After this group trinity ritual, we returned to No-Form, and then brought those elements and items of our ancestral legacy into our individual altars that we set up at the periphery of the workspace. These individual altars circled the entire workspace as a container we designated as "The Temple of the Ancestors". From No-Form, we entered The Temple of the Ancestors with the directive of visiting each altar as we moved through the space, taking in the shapes and presence there.

December 20, Winter Solstice

This lab finally culminated in a restoration of a sense of alignment with mystical realms of past, present, and future ancestral presences. The results of tonight's rituals were simultaneously sobering and liberating, leaving us all in a state of dynamic calm. We laughed, we cried, we sighed, and said good-bye. It was a good night.

The Mind is a Liar and a Whore

In the few months following this Lab, I continued reflecting on the earlier "Two-Faced Clowns" episode that resulted in such dynamic characterizations, characters that never found a home anywhere. I couldn't let it go. I was fascinated by this idea of hypocrisy as a source for a possible film. Over the following weeks, this potent seed-idea germinated into the premise of what would become my 2007 movie, *"The Mind is a Liar and a Whore"*—about a quirky household of roommates in citywide lockdown during an alleged bioterrorism attack over Christmas. I saw each of them freaking out, not about the alleged attack itself, but about their preconceptions of what was happening. Observing the folly of my own preconceptions—how they never could truly match the actual situation they were prefabricating in my head—I decided that all preconceptions were lies of the mind. Not just any mind, but *the mind that is a liar and a whore.*

The "SONG & PRAYER Lab" Autumn 2006
October 1–December 18; Three months
Culminating in "WHEREABOUTS UNKNOWN"
Our First Public Lab Witnessing; Finn Hall

Lab Intent Interrupted

We started this Lab by attempting to learn an early Armenian choral work as the basis for developing the more advanced paratheatre skill of "ritual actions," the precise and repeatable movements expressing the essence and feeling of the song as it's sung–*embodied voice work (State of Emergence,* p. 56). Our intention was to learn the song, find the ritual actions, and perform the results in public performance after three months of practice. However, discovering the intersection of song and ritual actions of this particular song proved beyond our present talents and skill sets. Too ambitious; we were in over our heads.

About five weeks into this Lab, I chose to drop our original intent. I felt we simply did not have enough time to do justice to this ritual song experiment. Though we continued practicing elements of the song and movement modality of the ritual actions, the intent shifted towards an exploration of various prayer forms, such as silent prayer, movement prayers, and "long distance sending" prayers that were projected beyond the time and space continuum to faraway others.

Though we were disappointed by the collapse of our original intent, this shift towards prayer-forms felt organic and somehow important. We continued in this prayer vein for the following five weeks with good results, until this intent shifted once more to a more open-ended intention of "approaching the unknown." During the final few weeks of this Lab, nobody knew what was going to happen next, or where we were headed with each session.

We agreed, albeit in various degrees of unspoken resistance, to approach Uncertainty as a direction in and of itself–uncertainty as a creative state. I arrived at each session free of preconceptions about what directions to suggest, and placed my full faith in intuition to guide each night. My aim was to sustain receptivity to the group spirit whichever way it went or wanted to go. Approaching the unknown in this way eventually liberated us from needing more structure or previously planned directions to do the work. We were free-floating babes in the abyss, taking on whatever happened.

Participants

Sylvi Alli, Julian Simeon, Jojo Razor, Nick Walker, Robin Coomer, Antero Alli, Joshua Bewig, Kate Gibson, Alaska Yamada.

"Whereabouts Unknown"

We unanimously agreed to culminate in a Public Witnessing of our final lab session, an event I titled, *"Whereabouts Unknown"*. We were clear that this was not to be a performance *per se*, but just another Lab session. We would also do this as our final Lab session, whether any witnesses showed up or not. We agreed not to consciously plan anything for the night beyond our usual preliminary warm-up procedures. I would, as before, call out the ritual directions based on my intuitive responses in the moment. As most of the participants of this lab were seasoned Lab veterans, I felt confident enough in our levels of individual and collective autonomy and integrity to handle whatever came up.

The Public Witnessing Event

From the genesis of this Paratheatre medium in 1977, there was never an audience to witness our private Labs...until now. Twenty-years later marked the first ever Public Witnessing of a Lab session, and it could not have mirrored a more vivid example of unknown outcomes. About sixty or so people flooded into the workspace while we were halfway through our physical warm-up. This overflow of seating capacity at Finn Hall significantly buffers the rich, "wet" acoustics we were previously accustomed to. Our vocals lost their previous luster and resonance. Maybe five witnesses arrived either drunk and/or MDMA-drenched. Throughout the event, these five erupted in spontaneous chanting, talking, and outright sobbing until one of them got up and raged out the exit door, screaming.

All the while, our commitment and focus deepened, as it had to, through the group polarities of Cultural Static and Planetary Source, Love and Fear, and finally culminating to group ritual prayers—from silent prayer to the transmission of *sending prayers* to the witnesses. Afterwards, we convened in the center of the workspace—as has been our custom—and shared notes with each other as the sixty or so witnesses listened on. We then opened it up for questions from the audience of witnesses. Everybody remained in the room with us for an hour until around 11pm when they started wandering out.

The days following this public witnessing were difficult for me. I had the feeling we had stepped into a circle of vulnerability meant to remain private, and not placed under the gaze of a hundred prodding eyes. This had never happened before. This was the first time we had invited anyone, let alone a full-house audience to audit an actual Lab session. This was a significant mistake. I learned that any public presentation of the utter nakedness of this work requires a formal container—a structure—to bridge audience and performer. What led me into this error? I think I needed to experience firsthand the specific and necessary limitations of how to present this paratheatre work to the public, and now I know. More on this later…

The CHAKRA Lab—Spring 2007
8 Monday Nights, 3/12–5/30, Finn Hall

Lab Intent

This Lab explored more advanced work with seasoned ritualists. Our focus was accessing, embodying, and giving physical and vocal expression to each of the eight chakras—energy centers in the Body (seven within us, and one above the head). We looked to the direct experience of the energies radiating from within each chakra to guide us, rather than any preconceptions of their meaning or function as described in esoteric books. Each chakra was explored in the following week-by-week sequence: 1, 5, 2, 6, 3, 7, 4, and 8.

Participants

Sylvi Alli, Jojo Razor, Nick Walker, Julian Simeon, Antero Alli, John Doyle, and Robin Coomer.

Four-Part Lab Session Structure

The internal landscape of sources proved amongst the more subtle of my paratheatre experiences so far. Subtle, as in detecting the faint emanations originating from the body's own ley lines and power spots, the Chakras. These energies cannot be forced or manipulated. Great receptivity is required just to begin detecting their emanations, and why this Lab constitutes advanced paratheatre work (all the participants were seasoned vets). The space was dark with our only source of illumination being single candles at the north and south walls.

A 4-part lab structure emerged during our first week (the root chakra), that was applied to each of the following weeks, making slight adjustments to best serve the moment. Each session's aim was to explore that week's chosen chakra towards its embodiment and expression in movement, sound, and gesture.

After the 40-minute physical warm-up of each weekly session, I asked everyone to prepare their personal area for that week's chakra. From No-Form, we projected that chakra into our area, stepped inside, and waited to register the emanation. Sometimes the emanations hit right away; other times, we needed patience. This first ritual phase involved allowing that chakra's emanation to expand from its originating point in the body, and then throughout our entire body towards its full-on embodiment.

The second ritual phase of this Chakra lab structure involved a group polarity to accelerate the spin of each chakra. In the first week

(Chakra 1), we worked with the polarity of Safety and Danger; the second week (Chakra 5), it was Listening and Calling. In week five (Chakra 3), we engaged the polarity of "earth-body" and "dream-body" as experienced through the solar plexus.

The third ritual phase of each session had to somehow serve and challenge the activated and recently opened chakra. This phase took on different forms each week, depending on the specific chakra. The fourth ritual form involved designating the ritual space to the "realm of the god, goddess, or source" of that chakra. The intent here was to enter the workspace from No-Form, and find relationship with that chakra's source through sound, movement, gesture, and prayer while moving across the space. After the final ritual, we always met in an ending group circle to check in and share our impressions.

Week 1; Root Sacrum (1st) Chakra

Moving across the space as if under the skin of the earth. I felt enveloped and empowered, as if the skin containing me was also propelling me across the surface of mass; gravity as energy source. I discover the root chakra as the "foundation of all existence," and its presence expressed as love.

Week 2; Throat (5th) Chakra

Listening and Calling. Rapture erupts and ripples throughout my body as I commit to total listening. The call was a signal transmitted in the fog (a lighthouse?), developing into some version of my "calling" as a purposeful tone, as in my life's calling.

Week 3; Spleen (2nd) Chakra

Group polarity of "what is mine," and "what is not mine" were quite charged for me, yielding a strong felt sense of a legacy and dignity earned in my life so far. In the "not mine" area, a sobering awareness overtook me of very personal limitations around what I was not here to do or to become.

Week 4; Pineal Gland (6th) Chakra

I discovered the violence of vision (clairvoyance, prophecy) without compassion. I gave myself over to its fierce, forceful directives with sudden, fast movements, sharp rhythms, loud clapping of hands, short bursts of shrill shrieks. I began tempering its overwhelming power through gradual acceptance of and compassion for myself and others.

Week 5; Solar Plexus (3rd) Chakra

The group polarity of Triumph and Defeat revealed the victory of Great Spirit, and the defeat of whatever resisted it in a refreshing revelation of power that belonged to nobody. I suggested an additional polarity of Earthbody and Dreambody, which led to a potent exposure of their interconnection, finding one within the other. I experienced sheer delight navigating the ritual space guided solely by the vibrating fibers of my solar plexus.

Week 6; Crown (7th) Chakra

Vertical source jogs were used to align with the crown center. After the warm-up and personal area chakra embodiment, the space was divided between "Infinity" and "Identity" (not a polarity), with group

No-Form along the west wall. Then we entered the group polarity ritual "Entity That I am" and "Creature That I am," with No-Form along the east wall. Passing between these two zones yielded such depth, energy, and grandeur; words cannot do justice–simply astonishing. Infinity expands everything, while Identity captures strands of that luminosity, and creates forms, melodies, and movement designs within its vibrating containment. The final ritual of "god or source of the crown center" brought me to my knees with ecstatic vertical communion.

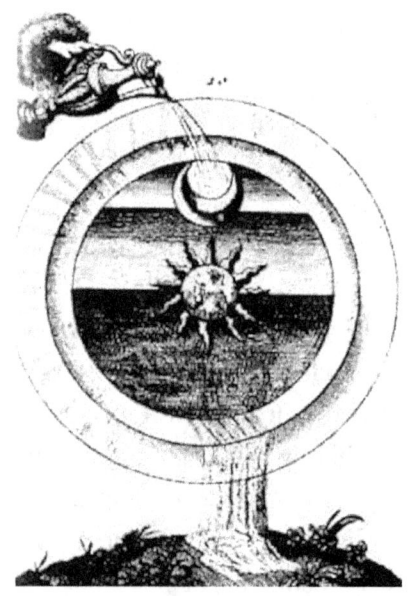

Week 7; Heart (4th) Chakra

We explored realms of the "broken heart" and "healing" (not a polarity), where I found a love renewed after letting go of a love that meant nothing to me anymore. The second pass into healing revealed my unexpected role as an initiate with a power to heal others. The group polarity of "the heart's desire" and "the heart's remorse" proved instructive, allowing me to participate more consciously in remorse as conscience-building ritual. Moving with and as "the Presence of Love" throughout the night reminded me of what I am truly made of—by expressing myself, I am expressing love.

Week 8; the 8th Chakra (3 to 5 feet above head)

After our physical warm-up, we individually explored the embodied expression of chakras one through seven, alone in our own personal areas. What unfolded for me was an intense serpentine eruption. With all seven chakras now opened up, we stepped into the group polarity of "Embodiment" and "Disembodiment"; this exposed for me the out-of-body context of the 8th chakra, where consciousness slipped out of linear time and space towards the non-locality of singularity; the subtle weirdness of non-duality.

Then, we formed a group No-Form circle (backs to center), while postulating a sphere suspended one to five feet above the group circle. I suggested that we fill the sphere with either gold, silver, or violet energy (in accord to preference), and then draw a line of this energy down through our crowns to fill and animate our bodies. This ritual was for me the most profound. Molten gold light flowed down through my bones, my veins, my intestines, my muscles, as I gasped for air while singing praises to the source of this mysterious power.

We then relocated to the periphery of the space, initiated the hollow No-Form technique, while designating the entire space to the sphere itself; we then re-entered the space to navigate through the ephemeral sphere of energy now expanded to fill the entire workspace. This ritual felt like a subtle integration of the 8th chakra, and a formal acknowledgement of its presence in my life.

In the group circle that culminated in this final Lab session, everyone confessed to having accessed the 8th center in some way or another. Many stories were shared. Gratitude was conveyed for the commitment we demonstrated these past eight weeks, especially to such subtle energy sources and their embodiment through physical and vocal expression.

DREAMING RITUAL Lab—Spring 2008
Entering the Mountain's Dreaming Vortex
Indoors 3 Months; Mount Tamalpais 3 Nights

Lab Intent

To develop a ritual choreography based on movements recalled from our night dreams *(State of Emergence,* p. 77), and then to perform these as dreaming rituals over three nights at Mount Tamalpais in Marin County, California. The ritual forms and sources introduced served the simultaneous development of two "bodies":

1) EARTHBODY–*executing the physical mechanics of the dreaming movement cycle (made up of three to five separate movements recalled from dreams) with increasing precision and flow, or grace.*

2) DREAMBODY–*accessing a network of vertical sources to activate the internal landscape, and catalyze and animate the physical dream choreography itself.*

This Lab saw a more dominant, internal focus with the values of solitude and verticality favored over one-to-one and/or group interaction. This was not an interplay Lab, but a committed immersion in solo dream choreography. Though moments of interpersonal interaction did occur, they were always within the context of separate, interacting dream choreographies, rather than any interpersonal interaction. An asocial climate was maintained by the persistence of spatial awareness initiating each session.

Final Ritual Night, Mount Tamalpais, May 19

Under a full moon, deep in the womb of a dense forest of towering redwood trees, our temple grounds were illuminated by seven candles and lanterns. The sources we served that night included: the *power of the Earth* where we stood, and the *power of the Dreaming* where we stood. Since these powers were already there long before we arrived, we had only to raise the heat in our bodies in the warm-up, and then cultivate enough receptivity via No-Form to engage these forces to animate our dream choreographies. Thanks to our prior seven weeks of working indoors (twice a week), these aims were met successfully, and we were now inhabiting the dreaming vortex of the mountain.

After seven weeks of emphasizing our separate dreaming rituals, a subtle yet profound group unity eventually emerged unexpectedly in this final ritual. But this was no unity forced by holding hands, or chanting together, or in any way contrived or improvised. This group unity erupted spontaneously as each of our separate dreaming rituals blossomed in each other's company, releasing subtle crosscurrents of a presence as palpable as our breathing, as whimsical as the astonished bemusement flickering across our fluid faces.

This experience revealed the intimate entwinement of the dreambody and the earthbody. What soon became evident was *the mountain was teaching us the dreaming*. This was dramatized after my surrender to the mountain geomancy of DEEP YIN within the profound magnetism of Mount Tamalpais. We were not merely moved or being moved by our own efforts alone. Our human ritual efforts in the warm-up, and our conscious surrender to the dreaming powers of the mountain, somehow raised the presence of Dreaming into our waking consciousness, moving us this way and that, in accord with *the telluric currents* we were riding.

I was shown that I cannot teach the dreaming. I can ask myself and others to remember movements from their dreams. I can provide opportunities, ritual techniques, and forms for bringing these movements into more precise expression. I can even play with summoning "dreamtime" presences and forces inside the four walls of our dance studio, perched on the second floor of a building in urban Berkeley. However, my personal strategies and urbanized ego fall short of any genuine transmission of the true presence of the dreaming that the mountain naturally transmits.

When I depend on my personal efforts alone, I easily slip into self-delusion and the belief that something great is happening. If I can lay down my ego and walk across it like a bridge to greater unknowns, no belief is required. A more direct experience led me to meet the mountain as *initiation*. This happened last night, and today I walk the earth calm, grateful, and spun.

The Invisible Forest

Over the following weeks, the lasting influences of our Mt. Tamalpais experience aroused a strong vision for my 2008 film, *"The Invisible Forest"*, about a theatre director who brings his troupe into the woods to explore French Surrealist Antonin Artaud's magic theatre of ghosts, demons, and angels. At first, I resisted portraying the theater director. It felt too close to home, and I was also hoping to find someone who could do it better than I could. I auditioned actors, and could not find anyone that was a good fit for the role. When the production was ready to move forward, I caved in and accepted the lead role. It was also my first time carrying the lead in any film.

After the movie was fully cast that summer, we returned to Mount Tamalpais as the story's primary set and setting. Without a screenplay, *"The Invisible Forest"* was to become my most experimental feature, entirely improvised with the exception of two scenes from

Sacred Rites

Shakespeare's "The Tempest" and "Romeo and Juliet" and Artaud's stunning "New Revelations of Being". Though I think I pulled off the challenge of playing the lead while also directing the film, it was pretty stressful and wasn't anything I wanted to repeat. After the premiere of *"The Invisible Forest"*, I took a three-year break from making films. During this time, my focus remained with the Dreaming ritual and related sources with the Muses archetype.

The MUSES Lab—Spring 2010
10 weeks; Monday & Thursday Nights at Finn Hall

Lab Intent

Participants in this Muses Lab *(State of Emergence,* p. 91) were all artist-identified individuals, motivated by the idea of discovering ritual forms and sources to inspire their Art beyond the workspace itself—as a singer, *butoh* performers, clown, actors. The experiment before us was to approach what I called a *Muses dialogue,* with the idea of "the Muses" as *autonomous archetypes that belonged to no one,* similar to the classic Greek mythology of *the daemon* (not demon). We also agreed to dismiss this archaic idea of having "my" Muse or "your" Muse and approached the experience as a mystery to discover whatever we could and how it might impact our creative and artistic lives.

Participants

Antero Alli, Sylvi Alli, Alaska Yamada, David Hunt, Adam Palermo, James Wagner, Todd Richmond, Michael Curran.

A Little Personal History

For the last 28 months, I have known myself as a kind of tunnelman, walking the *bardo* limbo zones marking the longest fallow period of artistic expression in my adult life. During this era of non-productivity, I discovered what I know, and don't know about creativity, surrender, patience, and faith. As it turns out, Creation never stops. Those passages of so-called non-productivity simply express a phase of a much larger cycle where it goes underground, creating the illusion that nothing is happening.

Fast Forward To: Session #16 of 20

At this point, all previous doubts have collapsed regarding the palpable numen of this autonomous archetype that the eight of us are courting. At first, the Muse was nowhere to be seen, heard or felt; now it has made a home near the edge of our group-mind where it was free to enter and exit according to its will. In our persistent appeal, the Muses found us appealing. My ego still throbs from last session's one-two suckerpunch of hot blessings and ice-cold slapdowns. Entering the Muses' dimension too naked, too open-armed, like a sheep to wolves, I felt slaughtered and slain—something I hope to never fully recover from. I entered their world wanting something, and learned that the Muses don't care about what I want. They care about offerings and gifts, what I can bring, and how I might best serve their agendas. I had to learn not to identify as "artist" or "creator," but as a vessel exploring a kind of nonverbal call-and-response dialogue with the Muses archetype. This is neither pretentious bullshit nor false humility, but a confession of my love for creation itself and the true artists working deep inside the engines of dark flow creation: *the Muses*.

Flashback

After the sudden death of my second daughter, Zoe, in late 1992, I was torn asunder and exposed to multidimensional sources of overwhelming tragedy and magic. The mingling of these forces fueled a nonstop run of film production for the next fifteen years, transforming Tragic into Magic with films as vessels for a heady mix of tragic insight and magical realism. After the premiere of my last film, *"The Invisible Forest"*, the Muse suddenly abandoned me, initiating a two-year passage through the *bardo* tunnels of non-productivity and undoing. Forced to relax my desire to create to simply walk the internal landscape—which was everywhere and nowhere—I became just another shining babe in the abyss. I think I know what Buddhists meant when they refer to the fertile void as true nature.

Back to Session #16 of 20

Having very recently exited this tunnel, I was finally walking into the Light, and was open to however Muse might make use of me. I wanted to appeal to them; I wanted them to find me appealing. In session #16 of this Muses Lab, a sudden revelation. I assumed that the previous Muse that transformed Tragic into Magic was done with me, and that another, new Muse would appear and guide me towards greater unknown horizons. In this session, a Muse did appear, but it was free of the power and magic of tragedy—this new Muse was radiating *white-hot joy.* There was no sobriety or gravitas to this Muse, but a very high level of play; extreme play, dangerous play...

I physically moved back and forth between these two sources I chose to explore these two Muses—*the dark flow and the bright radiance*—and discovered that I was, in fact, not leaving one Muse for another; I was becoming the bridesmaid of their wedding. These two Muses sought communion of their marriage within me. My body was to become an Alchemical vessel, their *vas hermeticum.* To prepare myself for this wedding, the Muses insisted that all my future approaches to their presence must first find expression in *trinities*—of sets of three sources that I had to engage physically, emotionally, vocally, and spiritually in a ritual dance of offering. It was also made clear, don't ask me how, that I could not enter their world wanting anything from them. Everything had to be presented as *an offering.*

I introduced this trinity source idea to the group as any triptych of sources showing strong resonance in our lives that would act as a bridge to the realm of the Muses. Through embodying these trinity sources in a vocalizing rhythmic ritual dance, we would approach the Muses while maintaining the integrity of our personal energy amidst the highly-charged, impersonal Muses presence where the Personal meets the Transpersonal.

In these rituals I uncovered three separate stories for a film I wanted to make, yet I was unable to move forward on any one of them. Since I don't like to force creation, I was patient. My highly observant partner, Sylvi, suggested I distill these three stories into my trinity sources in the Muses Lab. Good idea. I came up with: *Magician, Clown, Shaman.* Each of these archetypes link to entire worlds and stories, each with their own fates. I just did not know how they'd link up with each other, and had no interest in following any preconceptions (lies of the mind that is a liar and a whore).

The ritual space was dark except for four lit candles atop four separate pillars: three pillars formed a large triangle in the room; the fourth candle/pillar was placed in its center and designated to the Muse. Everyone worked their own separate trinity in this trinity temple by traversing the pathways between each of the three outer pillars/sources. Our intention was to journey through all the pathways to connect with each of the three sources, feeling the process of leaving each source behind and approaching the next source in a continuum of visiting our trinity.

Magickian > Shaman > Clown > Magickian

The Magician revealed itself as a source of knowledge and vision. Here there was repose, study, and clarity of architecture and universal design. While leaving it behind and approaching the Shaman, it felt like I was walking backwards in time, centuries with each step, to the originating source of magic—the Son pays homage to the Father. The Shaman revealed a source of wisdom and power. Here I immediately united with the living Earth. The animal, plant, and mineral kingdoms became my allies that I now embody to fulfill my purpose in service to creation. What is really happening here? I move on without an answer.

While leaving the Shaman behind and approaching the Clown, it felt like I was becoming human for the first time. The Clown revealed a source of joy and folly. I danced and yodeled the goofball celebration of the fool I was, completely free to express myself. Slaphappy Human. While leaving the Clown behind and approaching the Magician, I became aware of squandering myself, and the need for temperance and sobriety. Once returning to the source of the Magician, I felt sorrow for the loss of the Clown's spontaneity, and I lamented the disconnection from the Earth that I felt with the Shaman. Too much knowledge took its own toll. There was unspeakable sorrow here from too much understanding.

As I left the Magician and walked towards the Clown, my innocence was immediately restored as unbridled joy that subverted all my heavy-hearted magical knowledge. In the Clown, I danced my goofy dance, sang my whacky song in a joyous cacophony of infinite chaos. The world was my circus. Walking towards the Shaman, I collapsed to the floor, slowly crawling in the dark towards the single flame before me. Yelps and squeals of wild animals filled the space above and around me as I slowly took on the form of a panther, sauntering into the central Muse-realm with stealth and hyper-awareness. Returning to the Shaman pillar, I rose and sang my heart to the Earth. Leaving the Shaman behind and walking towards the Magician, I carried an ancient history of Paleolithic traditions connecting the

Shaman's archaic legacy with the Magician's modern views of the world. The offering to the Muses was taking hold and allowing me to continue dancing and singing, rather than slammed down for another pratfall faceplant. Happily, I chanted, *always a bridesmaid, never a bride.*

To Dream of Falling Upwards

The Muses Lab is over, and now the echoes begin. The waves of influences absorbed over the last twenty sessions settle and rise, descend and ascend, throughout my daily course of living. I find myself tending to a new inner action, a movement similar in feeling to the tiny convulsions of seedlings breaking ground as they reach for sunlight. This feeling informs my daily decisions about what to do, where to go, who to meet—and also around what, who, and where to avoid contact. Elements of a vision for a new film incubates deep within me. Something has taken hold, and is bringing me where I haven't gone before, just like how the Muses do...

The *bardo* tunnel-realm enveloping me for the last two years is gone. What's before me feels open and lit up. All the trinity source work in the Muses Lab has formed a kind of internal foundation from which I am discovering new contexts to view my daily experiences, and the artistic direction of this next film project. I start scripting the story within the next few days, initiating the effort to articulate what has been gestating within me. The trinity of Clown, Magus, and Shaman became the central pivot for the principle characters of Magickian Jack Mason and his two hot-headed apprentices he assigns the ego-corrosive ritual of going into business as Clowns. The Shaman appears here as a desert witch—or *bruja* (partly inspired by the three desert witches in Castaneda's books)—whose rural sorcery tests the Magickian's urban magick. The screenplay for *"To Dream of Falling Upwards"* practically wrote itself over three delirious, whiskey-soaked nights.

RITUAL ACTIONS of the MUSES Lab
Mondays & Thursdays, Dec. 20–Feb. 10, Winter 2010–2011

Lab Intent— "Ritual Actions"

We practiced a skill in this Muses Lab called *ritual actions (State of Emergence,* p. 91). It develops through three stages of source work that can give expression to the innate *function and purpose of any given source* without imposing any ideas about what that might be or look like. Ritual actions mark an advanced Paratheatre method for bridging ritual into performative, experimental theatre, as explored earlier in *Orphans of Delirium* (2004), *Requiem for a Friend* (2005), *Songs as Vehicles* (2005), and during the Portland Productions (2016–2018).

Identification

The first stage involves cultivating enough internal receptivity—via No-Form practice—to detect, engage, and merge with the source itself. Identification expresses a conscious act of surrender to the source as full-bodied, immersive experience. The results can be chaotic, convulsive, ecstatic, yet without communicating anything beyond catharsis.

Service

In the second stage, there's a shift from merging and identifying with the source towards serving its directives. This shift can clarify the expression of patterns, characteristics, and rhythms innate to that source, resulting in increased economy of movement and clarity of form in whatever forces are engaged and served.

Sustaining Care (Empathy)

The third stage moves into a discovery of what we care most about—or love most about—any given source we are engaging and serving. This happens in the moment we engage the source from No-Form, rather than from any preconception of what we think we care about or love. As we commit to this experience, we can discover a *sustaining care of empathy* that nurtures and informs the quality and expression of whatever source we are engaging and serving. As the source expresses itself through our empathy, so then can the audience in a performative setting feel it as well.

Session 1: 12/20/2010

Starting on the lunar eclipse, Winter Solstice night, set a tone of anticipation in me around our journey to meet the Muse. Of the eight of us, five had undergone the first Muses Lab (Spring 2010); the other three are seasoned newbies that I felt were ready to advance themselves. So far, this feels like a solid group. I decided to return to the two primary structures that did us well in the first Muses Lab: 1) working with charged trinities and 2) conducting our individual warm-up cycles in the same spot for all sixteen sessions.

The primary difference in this Muses Lab would be the advanced Paratheatre method of "ritual actions"—movements sourced by the Muse archetype that articulate its innate purpose through us. How are we being used by the Muse to express its purpose? We are courting the Muses as vessels and mediums to communicate their agendas through us via physical stillness, motion, sound, song, gesture, and ritual actions.

Working with Trinities and "Body as Unit"

My trinity tonight was Sky, Human Being, and Earth. After passing through this trinity in my solo ritual, we all passed through our separate trinity-sources collectively while focusing on the Body As Unit technique, a process for engaging the whole body in motion as one piece; picture a cat moving across the floor. Body As Unit shows how to move in ways that maintain a felt sense of unity in motion so that no part of our body remains isolated or divided from the rest. This technique expands range of motion. We also explored the contact point of finding and giving expression to the purpose or function of each of our three trinity sources.

Towards the end of our 3-hour session, and after our collective trinity work, the room was set up for approaching the Muse Archetype. Passage towards the Muse realm involved first immersing ourselves in a ritual integration area, opposite to the Muses area, and dedicated to the fluid embodiment of our trinity as three moving parts. This integration area also served us as a base of familiarity to return to after the potentially more extreme, volatile, and unpredictable Muse realm. It also gave a personal context to the Muses, since we were entering from our trinity integration zone where we were already immersed before entering the Muses area.

When I first entered the trinity integration zone, I felt lost. What was I doing here? I began remembering the earlier movements expressing the function of each of my three sources: Human, Sky, and Earth. Doing these movements helped me feel ready to cross over into the Muses realm. But after passing over into the Muses realm, something in me immediately froze up. I felt locked inside my body. Immobilized! From this deep freeze, I gradually yielded to slow, almost majestic, physical motions, and a low, piercing, and sustained vocal—visually, I was standing, adrift and suspended, inside a clear blue iceberg.

Several very long moments later, I found my way back to the familiar trinity integration zone, now revealed as a zone of self-work. A sobering revelation. I needed far more integration time with my personal trinity before returning to the Muses if I was to discover anything beyond the impersonal iceberg holding me captive like some prehistoric mosquito trapped in amber…yes, I need more time in the trinity integration zone.

Session 2: 12/23/2010

Tonight's session began with presence actions, a technique for increasing a palpable, felt sense of one's own energy as a field or aura. This process was then challenged by limiting all our movements to walking backwards, and then sideways, and then forward. The final transition of this cycle had us exploring an omnidirectional way of moving—forwards, backwards, sideways—while giving moment-to-moment expression to our felt presence. Doing this effectively expanded my range of motion while preparing us to meet the demands of the Physical Warm-up Cycle already warmed up.

After the Physical Warm-Up cycle, I felt compelled to return to the last session's trinity of Sky, Human Being, Earth. This time, I didn't hold back; I gave myself fully to each source. In EARTH, I engaged a power of maximum density that concentrated my entire being. All I could do to not explode was to begin singing this song of the Earth with my entire being, a song without words that buzzed my vocal cords like some hungry, Tuvan throat-singer.

Stepping into HUMAN BEING source allowed a greater circulation of that EARTH force, opening my heart and extending my arms into a repeating pattern that shifted between fighting and seeding, between warrior and farmer, in an ongoing expression of HUMAN purpose acting through me now: *fighting and farming*. Stepping into the SKY source, my arms were gently lifted upwards in a gesture of giving everything away. Whatever I had achieved through fighting and farming, I was now giving up to the SKY.

Sacred Rites

The Muse Approaches

Standing in No-Form at the eastern wall, facing the western wall designated to the MUSE realm which was framed by three pillars with lit candles. Between east and west, each of us defined our own pathway, or lane, to approach the Muse three times—each pass incorporating one of our three trinity sources—and return to the east wall in No-Form. On my first approach, I was alarmed by the sudden electric charge triggered between my SKY source and the MUSE. Like the synapse gap between neurons, the space between these two sources sparked an avalanche of kinetic energy. All I could do to stay intact was perform the upwards arm movements innate to my SKY source with all the commitment I could muster. This energy was not mine to keep, but to give away to the SKY.

The second pass aroused the fighting/farming patterns of the HUMAN BEING to the MUSE, whereupon it was made clear what I was fighting for and what I was seeding. I was fighting for the MUSE, and seeding its influence wherever it could take root—the HUMAN BEING was clearly in service to the MUSE. The third pass through the EARTH to the MUSE revealed a totally impersonal function for grounding the charge, much like how the Earth absorbs lightning strikes in an electrical storm.

The rest of the night found us integrating these three sources towards a fluid whole or cohesion, an innate pattern of motion we brought into the MUSE realm. The idea was to discover the purpose of our 3-prong pattern. Recalling last week's failure, I chose to commit more time and concentration in this integration self-work zone before crossing over to the MUSE realm. My patience paid off. I was able to navigate throughout the MUSE realm without becoming obliterated or losing touch with myself, my trinity ritual dance. The purpose of my pattern? To be used by the MUSE in whatever way it dictated while maintaining my integrity. The artist in me found this useful. Serve the Muse without destroying myself—easier said than done. My work is clearly cut out for me.

Session 3: 12/27. Embodied Voice Methods

Tonight our group work began with an embodied voice method inspired by Sylvi. This technique involves a three-step process: 1) sourcing a given energy, 2) resonating a sound that matches its frequency, and 3) allowing the vibration of that sound to dictate physical movement. Motivated sound as movement resource. With practice, sound and movement blend and are unified. This process was applied through each source of my new trinity (Earth, Water, Air) as an unbroken tone that underwent pitch shifts as it passed through each element. On the second pass through our trinity sources, we distilled our expressions by holding ourselves to only moving as far as the vibration of the tone dictated. This adjustment minimized the wailing melodramatic sounds we heard in the first pass by the restraint of *movement economy*.

Before entering the Muses realm, we designated a preliminary area to engage a new source through the embodied voice process explored earlier to stabilize a sound/movement pattern to bring to the Muses. My source was FIRE. After establishing the presence of Fire in sound and movement, I entered the Muses realm. I was gently startled. My fire was not blown out or exaggerated, but dignified by the Muses. A thought surfaces. As the force of inspiration circulates and transmits through me, so then may I inspire others. A humbling revelation: inspiration belongs to nobody, yet touches all.

After that ritual, we chose one source from our personal trinity that we felt might be most in harmony with the Muse. Among Earth, Water, and Air, I chose Earth. After establishing its presence in sound and motion, I brought this process to the Muse. I found myself immediately gravitating to each of the four corners of the Muse area and making myself useful by articulating actions and gestures of containment. The Earth element was in harmony with the Muse by providing substance, form, and structure for its expression. I was left feeling deep gratitude for the simple act of being useful, and was moved to prayer. I was not praying to anything or anyone as much as giving physical and spiritual form to my gratitude for being useful.

Session 4: 12/30/2010

I initiated this session by calling a group circle to discuss the nature of the sources we chose to work with. I asked, *"What is the difference between a source and a force?"* I offered the example of the physical body as a source unto itself that unleashes its own innate forces when felt deeply; the body as a source, not a force. I also shared my experiences around the high potential of self-delusion in this work—how easy it was to start mentally tripping-out, thinking that something was actually happening when we're only thinking about something happening. How to discover vital sources of energy beyond our mental constructs? I encouraged everyone to question their choice of sources, and to raise the bar by keeping these sources less abstract and more personally relevant.

Now it was my turn to put myself on the line. I added a new source with my trinity–"my relation with God"–and soon rediscovered the infinite power and love where it always was: within, around, above, and below me. When the group trinity work started, we applied the technique of sustaining care, effectively arousing a deeper emotional investment in each of our three sources and their corresponding patterns of motion. This method of sustaining care offered profound revelations I don't have words for. As the group trinity work progressed through the next pass, the Muse realm was added, up above overheads near the ceiling of this Masonic temple room. This allowed us to respond to the Muses from another angle–from below to the presence of the Muses above. Whoa...oh my gods...again, words fail me!

The final ritual had us approaching the Muse realm after a preliminary realm of the sustaining care method in our foundation source. Sustaining care for my relation with God was so fulfilling that it relieved me of any want or need for the Muse. Cradled in this God-love, I entered the Muse realm wanting nothing. What happened next took me by surprise. Wanting nothing yielded a bounty of imagistic wealth–golden-hued god-forms, and transparent bird-like creatures languished throughout this Muse temple, all aglow from within. I sat crouched, eyes closed, one arm raised with the other angling down to the floor. In the stillness of this repose, I witnessed a delicate unfolding of faintly luminous outlines of what seemed to be archetypal entities coming and going around me.

By wanting nothing, I was left alone. It felt as if I had temporarily become one of them, or at least invisible enough not to be bothered with. All this proved a bit much for me as I stood up, left the Muse realm, and returned to No-Form.

Session 5: 1/3/2011

This session began with exposing our personal movement clichés, those kinetic patterns typical and predictable to each of us. I asked the group to cut loose, and start busting up our too clever-to-cute moves until we embarrassed ourselves, and got it out of our systems; good liberating fun. The rest of the session incorporated the technique of service to our trinity of sources which then led to giving expression to the innate purpose or function of each source—what I call *ritual actions,* the new skill we were learning in this lab.

My trinity tonight was Power, Love, and Vision. Each offered very different source points for their idiosyncratic patterns of motion and actions. In Love, I melted into the center of myself and could only spin softly, arms outstretched, serving Love as a conduit for its transmission. Upon entering Power, my body immediately contracted—sprouting legs, thighs, feet, torso, arms, neck, and a head! The shape of my human form was apparently obliterated by the power of Love, and now reclaimed by the love of Power. The function of this Power source was to simply get things started, as ignition and combustion—my movements served this as directly as possible. Passing through Vision, I suddenly dropped to the floor in a slump. Here, I rose slowly to a vertical stance of utter stillness where omnidirectional awareness rotated my body towards a 360-degree scan of the workspace. I resonated a singular, low tone to this slow circling as my sole reference of self. I returned to No-Form.

THE JOURNALS OF OTHERS
Trained in this Paratheatre Medium
Leah Kahn, John M. Doyle, Paradox Pollack, Sylvi Alli, Jessica Woletz, JoJo Razor, Nick Walker, David Hunt, Jesse Bockler, Brendan Ramsden, Serene Zloof, Jakob Bokulich, James Wagner

In response to this mostly nonverbal, visceral, and emotional work process, these Lab reports supported the psychological integration of the immersive, in-depth, intuitive experiences with context and meaning. After the year 2000, the ritual journal became an integral part of Paratheatre training for myself and others. — A.A.

The ANIMA/ANIMUS Lab, 2001
by Serene Zloof (aka DatGirl)

To The Universal Law of Attraction—whenever I'm getting some (attention), everyone I encounter suddenly wants my attention. They can sense the intimate energy seeping through the skin; they can feel a sexuality that is fully engaged, and all are drawn to it. Equally, when I'm out of touch with these forces, it becomes even harder to draw touch towards me. It may seem like a cruel catch-22, but that is only if you believe, as I once did, that sexuality can only be explored with another person. Quite the contrary. I have discovered a very potent secret—intimate contact with male energy is not dependent on meeting a man. Not when is it possible to cultivate a relationship with the archetypal male force of the universe, the Animus, who exists within every man.

Sacred Rites

It begins with a call. The building of a virtual temple charged with my energy, a request for his presence, whatever that may embody. I found that my call to him included the sounding of three tones with my voice. As I went through the process of building a temple for the Animus to visit, it dramatically changed my life and the way I relate to men. During the Anima/Animus Lab, I discovered that the Animus encompassed all forms of man that I have known—brother, father, lover, son, and advisor.

My first experience with the Animus was childlike and playful: he visited me as the boy next door, and we stomped around the playground together like brother and sister. I felt myself embodying a boy, the Animus within me. The next experience we had made me feel completely female in his presence, for it was an interaction of primal sexuality. I felt the desire to be truly submissive, even to the point of humiliation and painful pleasure. Then I experienced the sexual side of female domination, where I was some cross between sensual mother and ravaging lover. It is truly fascinating that some of our meetings made me embody the force of woman, while others had the opposite effect of filling me with the male power to make and destroy.

The stage of the lab work that followed was one of teaching. The Animus became an older man, a father figure with a mustache. The image of Socrates comes to mind because the Animus was guiding me by responding to my questions with more questions. We began to have long written conversations, where my pen would speak his answers. Soon, all of my issues about being a woman in this society—the pressure to be a goddess on a pedestal, or a stand-by-your-man kind of gal—were dissolving.

I could choose any role I wanted to play, male or female; a strange invincibility. The Animus told me that there was a piece of him within every man. But even if there were never any men around, he assured me that he would always be there to satisfy my need for male companionship. Three weeks later, we were having a written conversation. I asked, "Am I really ready to share my life with someone, and how much will I share? Everything? Even our conversations?"

The Animus wrote back, "It's up to you what you choose to give. It is whatever you want it to be." Someone walked into the room just then. The One I would marry in a few short years. Neither one of us knew that at the time. In fact, as our intensity together rapidly elevated like wildfire, he was overwhelmed and could not continue being intimate with me. So, we did the declaration of "just friends." Disappointed, I was, BUT in the grand scheme it didn't matter! He was just one face of the Animus, and there would be another.

I detached easily, to his surprise. And a few weeks later I had a hot date—with the Animus. I got dressed up to go out, decorated my space, and built the temple—and sure enough, I received enough male energy to feel satiated. Just as our meeting was over, the phone rang. An old lover of mine inviting me out. Then the phone rang again, and guess who it was? "Just Friends" was over. Hmmm... Imagine that.

"Orphans of Delirium"
Journal Entry by Paradox Pollack, 2004
On the public performance following the Initiations Lab

Antero wants me to play a half-man, half-woman, but I don't feel that. A demand for life arises—a pushing out of my skin that has no limit.

What has come to me is a direct confrontation with the child I was when I believed, somehow, that I died in the fire at 14 years old. When I was caught inhaling smoke, I left my body for 10 minutes. What comes to me is a coiling of a heated metal that I shape by my breath. A denial of death.

My movements balance between the black ore of my left hand and the heated forge of my right. It is not imagination that guides me; it is not listening to the others as they howl like the beasts in the underworld. Instead, it is my own life pounding in my belly that, like a snake sloughing off its skin, each time I find a repetitive movement to surrender to.

Under the banner of the Ancestors, the wind passes through me; bellows that fuel the flame I have been cultivating. A swirling up and ever-spinning sears my organs and flesh. I am a beast of loam coming from the earth, a Golem I am creating to save the life in me that is dying. As if I could master this action, renew myself, and fight the death that will one day retake me.

Now I am that beast. I have made a cycle of it. An entire season of shaping this set of conditions, sculpting this fusion of fate that I cannot control, and I no longer recognize myself.

First, the dreamer who walks into the world of the dreamers, and with my top hat, calls the circus of the *Bardo* to arise. The most subtle mists come through me, and I am committed to waking and The Dreaming. But as soon as I have walked through the mist and seen the faces of the audience, I set to the ritual of caking myself in mud, curling clay into my hair, and becoming a demon that will not give up the life that the Sailor of the seas of Delirium has sacrificed himself to.

Each night I come to this same place, this place with no time and no position, just the fire and commitment that is a gas fire that bubbles up from a swamp, and burns away all regret and all confusion. Each night I use all of the force within me to combat the forces within this man who is killing himself. Each night I lose the battle.

"Orphans of Delirium"
Journal Entry by Jakob Bokulich, 2004
On the public performance following the Initiations Lab

There are all kinds of entertainment out there, and I don't know if what we did qualifies as any kind, but I can say without pretense that I don't believe anyone came away from what we did unmoved. Antero calls it a ritual—a word that I would only use with caution, because it's loaded with religious connotations. Then again, maybe it's appropriate, because often when someone digs down to the bottom of what they're feeling, they uncover a kind of religious or spiritual sentiment. And getting to the bottom of what we're feeling—I think that's what we did.

We weren't so much performing, as allowing the audience to bear witness to an experience... I don't know what was going on in other people's heads, but I was striving to penetrate through layers of myself, my ideas and my reality, to something more authentic, more immediate. To ignite into pure experience—mediated as little as possible by the mind and its concepts—and to build the greatest possible receptivity to pure physical sensation and impulse, like an electrical charge in my body or animal instinct.

We met twice a week for about four months, a diverse group of people, most with theater and movement backgrounds such as clowning, *butoh*, acting, singing, Capoeira, boxing, aikido, yoga, and kung-fu. We didn't even introduce ourselves by name for the first month, but as each of us committed ourselves to the process of the lab, we got to know each other in ways that we normally never would.

Like actors embodying different characters, we surrendered our bodies to simple ideas that are real and palpable to our lives—the four elements: dream, nightmare, loved, abandoned, etc.... We didn't try to demonstratively portray these ideas, and we tried to avoid even reacting to these ideas. If you will, it was like we tried to channel them as forces or energies at work inside our bodies.

During one of the "performances," I remember moving across the floor next to my friend Paradox, doing who-knows-what kinds of movements and sounds. A delirious laughter erupted from someone in the audience, and it kept on going and going. I think somewhere in the back of my head a self-conscious voice had something to say about it, but I wasn't listening to that voice. Instead, with Paradox, I approached the sound of the laughter, like two moths gravitating towards vibrations in the air, its waves moving our bodies...and the

Sacred Rites 147

laughter kept going and going, filling the room, from this person who was no longer an audience member, but a participant in our ritual...

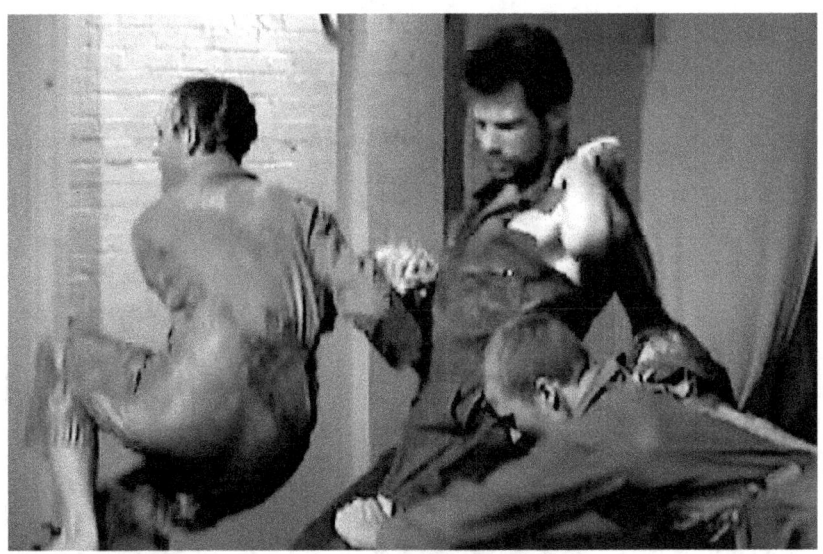

Often, as I go about my day-to-day stuff, I feel like I've only woken up half-way for the day, interacting with the world like a somnambulist. The only times I'm not just going through the motions, and that my eyes feel really open, seem to be when I'm performing, or in the *Capoeira roda,* or making art, when all of my attention is in focus. In "Orphans of Delirium" we went into trance-like states. This can be felt, watching the movie. That I think is interesting, though, it isn't so much the trance we went into as performers, but how—by juxtaposition—it makes me aware of the trance that I live most of my life in...

"ORPHANS OF DELIRIUM"
Performance/Video
*Production Notes by Antero;
May, 2004, San Francisco*

Stereotypes of "ritual"–pomp, rote actions, formality–were left behind early on in these experiments, and replaced with a more fluid, metamorphic approach. We were after something more alive. With the exception of the repetitive motions in the second ritual (recalled from participants' nocturnal dreams), none of the rituals were staged or improvised. Something else was happening here.

These paratheatrical experiments unfolded in their own cycles through sometimes gentle, sometimes violent eruptions, nudging and jolting participants to gesture, action, sound, interaction. These eruptions emanated from the body's own responses to the triggering of energy sources innate to itself, sources everyone was working to serve, embody and surrender to. The results were unpredictable and run the physical/emotional gauntlet. We never knew what was going to happen next. Just when we thought nothing was happening, nothing actually *was* happening, and then: boom! shriek! sigh...another eruption.

The live performances documented in this video followed four months of working with a primarily *naïve* group; naïve, meaning new to this medium. The first two months we worked without knowing whether or not we would perform. By releasing the pressure to perform, we were free to create our own pressures that eventually dictated the performance direction.

The themes emerging from our explorations—*initiation, vertical intoxication, shock*—expressed the emerging needs of this group animal, needs that informed all the ritual designs and sources. I was also committed to serving a group unity born, not from any blending of everybody's energies (which could produce an unwanted, sloppy, soup effect), but from how each participant's fight for their own integrity amidst forces—from within and without—that might otherwise consume them. Sometimes this fight was victorious; sometimes defeat had its way with the group.

To me, what matters most is the fight itself, not fighting against anything, but the good fight for one's consciousness within a maelstrom of chaos; a drama reflecting, for me, the heroic struggle to sustain their individual voice amidst society's deafening cacophony of conformity. This video provides a rare glimpse into this process.

TECHNIQUE Lab Reports, Spring 2005
by Leah Kahn, John M. Doyle, Sylvi Alli

Lab Intent

Our focus here was with the cohesive ritual technology of trigger methods *(State of Emergence,* p. 49) for catalyzing experiences of the internal landscape, while exposing redundant mannerism and movement clichés towards developing a sense of freshness by discovering our own idiosyncratic movement signatures. – A.A.

Leah's Lab Report

Devices... holding onto them and not holding on to them. having more than one, the option, a file cabinet of devices, a tool belt...all were beneficial, and becoming aware of something as a device was the key to entering the process of changing it, throwing it out, etc....

Movement stretch... difficult at times, to feel that i was actually in motion if i was to sustain the stretch long enough to enter into it deeply...movement being relative. continued awareness of moving through each stretch, though, was an aid to not fall into the sedation that some stretches can bring...

Rises... i especially loved the rises. sometime using only momentum, sometimes discovering different anchors where "strength" was not required. it was for me a method of letting go of muscles and moving from the bones...a sort of zen experience, where premeditation seemed to have no place.

Conversion from being to service... very significant... i did in fact truly experience the polarities as well as the conversions. where experience of being was true immersion, service was a bit more cerebral and analytical, like using a pair of scissors. by not being the thing, i found i focused on the actions rather than the emotional triggers that brought out an immersion into being.

Jogging... good for breaking the trance. sometimes it did not break trance, though, and other times it was a great way to let out any residual tension, emotion, confusion, etc. by using toning and sounds.... >even while riding my bike, i find many times when i reach the supposed limit of exhaustion, i suddenly begin toning and i move to the next level!< :)...i found No-Form jog strange, b/c it sort of ceased to be a jog...more of a walking meditation i suppose. non-directional and directional were helpful for me in becoming aware of patterns and breaking them, using effort and not using effort, creating heat or cooling down, etc. good for comparison and making differentiations. maintenance jog was very good for me to keep the energy going and still move into different phases or head space/body space...bridge the gap between worlds travelled.

John's Lab Report

Some of the devices (or techniques) that I resonated with were familiar from previous labs. In particular:

— **No-form**, which I now can relate to experiencing the core support and minimal effort around the internal "Rolf" line. What was also new here was moving from personal to "impersonal" No-Form... like crossing a lake, and then suddenly facing this unexpected and vast ocean, where all the unrecognized effort in "achieving" personal No-Form dropped away...

— **Prayer Circle** (especially finding a vocal tone that expresses connection and disconnection with source.)

Others devices were quite new for me, especially resonating tones and working with melody:

— discovering/letting the melody simply arise, rather than forcing/making it happen. Finding the Silent Source helped me in this.

— resonating tones in upper/middle/lower chambers.

A lot of the lab has been a time of "experiential anatomy" for me—exploring my spine...the contrast between comparatively slow and supportive bones, faster, more reactive/contractive muscles, and the superfast web of nerves that mediates between them. I also found a lot of "personality" differences between the left and right sides of my body (like Father and Son). Also, how they are unified, especially across the chest and through the heart.

Sylvi's Lab Report

There were a number of techniques that we worked with in this lab that I found quite valuable. I will address a few of them here.

"continuous, moving stretch" Employed in the pre-warm-up section, I found particularly valuable for the way that this direction encouraged me to find new ways of moving, stretching my body. I was surprised by the focus that it demanded, as well as how much it moved me out of the mental realm and more into the physical realm.

"trinity of movements" this was a new approach to a technique I was familiar with previously, but in the context of working with dream movements. It was quite interesting to apply this stitching together of movements into a looped "choreography" using movements discovered in a waking state, rather than in a dreaming one. I quickly found that I had a tendency to rush, to speed up the dance, but this led to exhaustion and "crazy-making" for me personally, forcing me to slow down. This technique really worked to develop my commitment to precision.

"searching for our melody" this technique totally amazed me. Starting in No-Form, we traversed the realms of sleep, wake, and dream, all the while looking for our melody, not forcing it, but maintaining receptivity to it, allowing it to emerge. When I found my melody, or rather, when it found me, I discovered the most effortless way of singing that I have ever experienced. It was truly mind-blowing.

"jogging through trinity sources" fascinating development of our No-Form jog. I was surprised at the subtle shifts in my physical movement as I traveled through the different sources. It was a good way to strengthen my sense of No-Form while in motion.

ALCHEMY Lab Reports, Spring 2006
Nick Walker, Sylvi Alli, Jessica Bockler, Jojo Razor
Ritual Mandalas & Wilderness Rituals

Lab Intent

To explore the archetype of The Self as a mandala through ritual forms and floor designs incorporating circles and spirals with a center and a periphery. For example, in one such ritual we imagined a large spiral filling the workspace floor. The center was designated to the Heart of the Self, and the periphery to the Ego. We'd start at the periphery in No-Form, and slowly spiral in towards the center, discovering how Ego might respond on its way to its possible defeat and final assimilation into the Self.

Ritual Mandalas

Mandalas were drawn during this three-month Alchemy Lab. Each mandala was created within 10–15 minutes immediately following the final ritual of each 3-hour Lab session. The only limits imposed were: 1) each mandala must have a center and periphery and 2) "keep it rough" by not to trying to create art as much as an honest expression of the internal state in the moment. I asked everyone to send me three mandalas from the twelve they had completed, along with any notes they wished to share. Five offerings are included here:

Nick's Mandalas & Notes

This is the only one of my mandalas for this lab that depicts recognizable figures rather than abstract designs. It had its genesis in the personal polarity I worked on that day: VENUS and MARS. In my natal chart, Venus and Mars are both conjunct my Sun, one on either side. This mandala represents the "Venus body" and the "Mars body" that I experienced in my exploration of the polarity (the Venus body is the one on top).

In this lab session, we explored the spectrum of colors. In the final group ritual of the day, each of us chose two colors as sources: one as the "cloak" that informed the way we moved through the shared space and interacted with others, and the other as the "essence" underneath that cloak, which we checked in with privately and occasionally revealed.

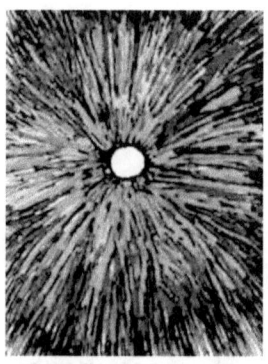

In this session we worked with the polarity of THAT WHICH EXTINGUISHES ME and THAT WHICH DISTINGUISHES ME. I came out of it with a gleefully radiant sense of the sheer joy of BEING, and I guess that's what this mandala is a picture of. I tend to leave blank, white space at the centers of my mandalas; perhaps it represents the ineffable Mystery at the heart of everything, or perhaps it's just No-Form.

Sylvi's Mandalas & Notes

This mandala emerged after a ritual session exploring the four elements.

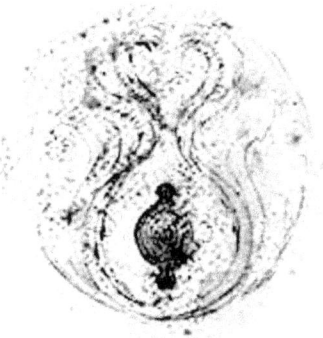

This was the only mandala that I drew when I was working apart from the group. I was laid up with a back injury and chose to do my own lab at the same time that the group was meeting. The mandala expresses what I discovered in working with the polarity of Desire and Need.

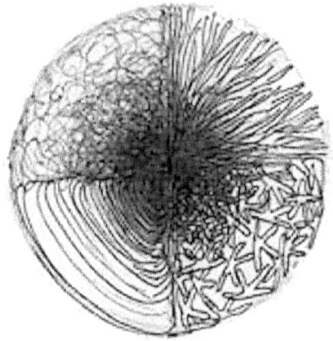

This mandala came after a ritual session exploring the four bodies—emotional, physical, mental, spiritual.

Jessica's Mandalas & Notes

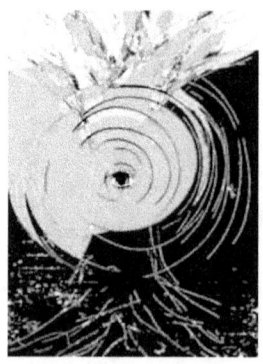

My commitment to serve vertical sources—which to me are those of the earth and those of the great beyond above. I am reminded of the tree of life. I commit and re-commit to my process of unfolding, and as I do, my connection to source strengthens and I become a stronger tree which may sway less in the motions of ritual and of life?

That which distinguishes Jessica is charged with such a diversity of voices! So many other me's! Oh, who is really me? Am I but a buzzing of fragmented identities? Am I one voice all at once? A being made of splintered me's?

The Body. Breath... flowing into blood... flowing into muscle... surrounding skeleton. One living system... made of many.

JoJo's Mandalas & Notes

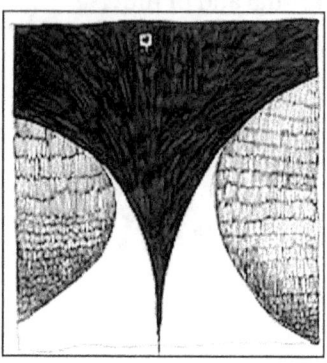

Realms of the Heart: This ritual began with a path splitting in two, forcing me into the underworld. The heart, a faint sort of hologram, floated above my head, and led me through a magical journey that included a boat ride down the Nile.

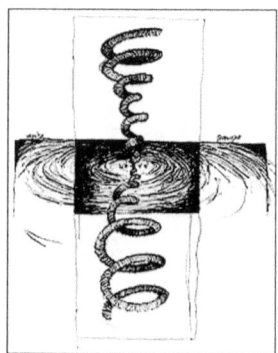

Impulse/Thought Polarity: After venturing into the extreme edges of impulse (over-stimulation) and thought (thinking to the point of non-movement), I eventually found a balance or center where I experienced a bliss-like quality in my being.

Sacred Rites   161

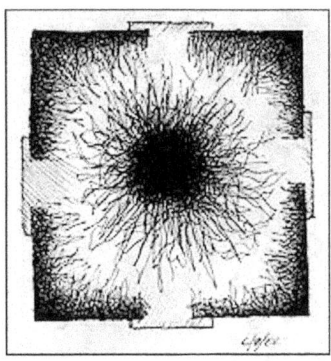

Source Mandala: Since all of my drawings were drawn after the rituals were over and the source had faded a bit, I decided to try to bring as much source into this drawing as was possible. I did not discharge the sources at the end of the ritual, rather invited them into the drawing experience with me. This was drawn mostly from my opposite drawing hand, and represents the four bodily arenas of the physical, spiritual, emotional, and mental.

Alchemy Lab, Wilderness Rituals, June 9–12

Occasionally, after an indoor training period, and depending on the Lab theme, participants have embarked to wilderness regions for three or four nights of telluric (geomantic earth-powered) paratheatrical ceremony. Over the years, we've ventured out to Orcas Island (Washington), Vidauwoo Wilderness (Wyoming), Shelter Cove and Mount Tamalpais (in northern California). The Alchemy Lab went to the Pinnacles Wilderness Park in central California over four days and three nights of ritual set in the beauty and power of its ancient (23 million years ago) volcanically-formed caves and terrain. No journal entries were shared during this trip.

After the final night ritual at Pinnacles

My experience with the rituals of our alchemy-based sources were strongly amplified by the power of the ancient volcanic soil and terrain there at Pinnacles. I felt a series of unexpected *seizes* the energy had over my body; not *seizures,* but this sense of freezing up in reaction to absorbing a previously unknown energy much bigger than my body. I worked with these *seizes* by giving them form as statues that I would allow to slowly come to life as my body adjusted to the shock with gentle convulsions and periodic release of tensions. After the final night ritual, the group energy was highly playful. Someone, I don't remember who, brought a bunch of hats, caps and headpieces with demon horns that we all put on for this ritual family photo.

Beginner's Mind Lab Reports, Fall 2007
by David Hunt, Jessie Woletz, Brendan Ramsden

David Hunt

My First Paratheatre Experience

This was my first experience with Paratheatrical Research. I came upon the information online while doing my own research around images and themes that had been coming to me in my daily musings. The information, essays, images, and ideas expressed sucked me in and down. As a performer, it resonated an approach I feel I had tasted in the most precious of moments while training–that is, technical and expressive work without attention to product, audience, or performance. On a personal level, the medium appeared to offer a space of exploration in areas in which I was currently grappling, namely the

Ladder of consciousness and awareness, the Shadow in all of its interpretations, and the path to know and change myself in my relationships with myself and the world around me.

Overview

The 8-week Lab was an experiential and technical introduction to the Paratheatrical medium. Its guiding thread was empowering the energetic body. Technically, the work happened through No-Form practice, exercises to develop personal and group devices to facilitate the ritual engagement with Source Energies, and facilitated rituals of Source Energy engagement. Personally, for me, the work called for commitment, courage, honesty, trust, and compassion. An overall journey into the understanding of integrity. Of course, I did not always answer to this call; it was very difficult, and at times, this call seemed—and may well be—completely mad.

The initial week's sessions revealed a deeper access, localization, and sensing of myself, my Energetic Body, simultaneously stimulating this/these Bodies and exploring my relationships to Source Energies, usually through polarization rituals. No-Form was the neutralization point, the starting and ending for all actions. No-Form provided a backbone to support the ventures in all directions. Equally central to the work for me was the ongoing challenge of directing my attention on the space itself, not on my ideas or feelings, but on what was outside of me.

As the sessions continued, the themes turned toward work in more personal areas of our lives, delving into the realm of shadows. Some of forces we approached included: Self Negation/Self Affirmation, Mother/Child/Father, Forgiveness/Blame, Goodness/Evil, Savior/Victim/Persecutor, etc. The final sessions addressed power loss and power gain. Where attention to Power Loss/Power Gain was present in many of the rituals, we met them directly through other sources—such as power loss and gain in Masculine/Feminine Energy, or head on as Sources unto themselves. The final rituals were set to confront our personal Demon that drains our power and seek ways to reclaim this energy.

I let myself be confounded. By directing my attention onto the space outside of myself with the intention to connect with specific forces, I discovered and witnessed new self-knowledge, greater honest emotional expression, and mysterious physical reactions. There is a likeness in every moment to a small green giant with glowing red eyes and manic hair whose cry is so wondrous and awe-full, and stinks of death so much you want to dance...aye this is the moment from where all goes...

Ritual Journal Excerpts

UNKNOWN SELF—response—there was pain, pain in the mystery. Monster? Grotesque?... Compelling to stay there. KNOWN SELF: "whimsical," sad, and fun; familiar. No-Form showed itself to be one of the most effective practices I've experienced for paring myself down to the moment. The sand slipping out of the glass, leaving a fullness of space and potential. Was aware of space as not empty... Mystery of experience; female face appeared again.

Left wrist. Backwards, counterclockwise movement, paddlewheel arms in Source of Life, giving... I need nourishment most now to engage in supporting that which needs to be destroyed, and that which needs to be created in my life. ...and while the movements approached some precision and repetitiveness, they elicited even deeper emotional and psychic (?) responses at times (not the first time that ritualizing brought my emotional body deeper and expressed more fully). I experienced an awareness and understanding of a transition happening from serving the Source, to understanding how it can, and sometimes does, serve me. Not always for the better. Is this my will, ego, essence? I'm confused... Space of the "SOUL"–devotion–that which moves and doesn't move; again, the spark behind the heartbeat, holding tissues together, the space between, the growth and impulse of trees, there is Source for me.

Jessie Woletz
The Mother-Father-Child Trinity

My experience working with the mother-father-child archetypes was subtle externally, yet powerful internally. Initially I was concerned that I was over-personalizing the categories, but the archetypes–they escaped me. At the time. I tried thinking of what the archetypes could be: dad–strong–yes; mother–caretaker, yes, but also strong; then I thought of father as weak. Child was easier to see as archetype. Child was vulnerable, yet protected by the parents. Child was experiencing the world freshly, and also through relationship to parents, in a way. Child was free to explore and learn, and also was fraught with disappointments of seeing reality, feeling injustice, frustrations, etc.

I gave into the three sub-personalities that arose in each section of the warm, candle-lit room. Being in the "mother zone" was a struggle–a loving one, but still very effortful to be in that position. So worthwhile though. No complaints in the energy expended; just a wish for more help. (A passive aggressive complaint? Or a surrender to the reality that I had to do it myself?) Eventually, mother carried a heavy cross, the burden of raising children. I couldn't resist thinking of my mother raising my sister and myself, as a single parent, the hard times she seemed to have gone through constantly, without the help of another parent. In my lab experience, being in this position was a lonely journey, that of the mother, but the heart-connection and intuition led the way. I could not separate my experience in this lab from my experience as a child raised by a single Mom, not knowing where my Dad was while in my adolescence.

Being a child in between the mother-father sides of the room was a bit of a relief. Not as heavy, but still holding great significance—or insignificance—as I struggle to separate these categories. In "child zone," I could roll around, sing a little, dance a little, feel free of responsibility, while remaining very dependent on others. The spirit of the child was invigorating in its innocence, and one I enjoyed returning to. In a way, I was a child in every zone, remembering my experience with my parents at a younger age, yet now experiencing what it would have been like to be in their place.

In father, I silently cried, my eyes poured tears; but again, it was subtle externally. Internally, so much was happening. A sadness, a very deep sadness, for my father who did not experience my or my sister's childhood. I felt I was experiencing what he went through. I wandered around feeling my children were missing, that I couldn't see them, they were lost in a void. All hope was lost in the world. I felt the absence of being a father to my children as if my soul had been ripped from within me. Once again, this is why I say I had a hard time sticking to the archetype.

My imagery of father-archetype kept shifting, initially to the point where I released my mind from trying to figure it out in order to give into the experience that was happening. I was reminded of conversations my Dad and I have had recently, now that we're back in touch, and he seemed to embody these emotions that I went through during lab, when describing what he went through during my youth. Same with my experience in the mother-archetype. I found myself being my Mom, going through what I thought she went through when raising us, from the way she described her experience. Eventually, I let go of wanting to separate from those personal ways of experiencing these "archetypes," sinking into my direct experience, allowing myself to move through, which ended up being the only way I could go.

The opportunity to interact was presented as an option, and I could not bring myself to approach anyone. Yet, someone found me, and put a hand on my back while I was slumped over in what is called *Paschimotanasana* in yoga (sitting forward bend). The hand was very reassuring. If I were not in lab, I would have responded differently; maybe thanked the person, looked up, moved away. But I stayed put. Did not offer anything in return, as I felt like it was more important to renew my energy, and OK to be selfish with it. I started to get up, and the hand reached out to help me, so I did not resist. Again, it felt odd to offer nothing back, only to receive this gift of assistance, but I went with it.

From this lab, I came away feeling a strong urge to talk to my family about the separation that still exists between my mother's and father's sides. I know I can't fix it fully or change what happened, but I was reminded of what a significant impact the past continues to have on the way we live our lives, and only by unearthing it more and letting it be released, do I feel I can fully come to the present and eventually move past it.

Brendan Ramsden

Working with Polarities

I was greatly inspired and supported by this group's resonant field of commitment to the work. I was very glad when Antero introduced a plea for Compassion and Devotion in the beginning stages of the work. With an ego as big as mine, I'll admit I considered the possibility that he was mostly wary of a lack of compassion from me! Anyway, the Devotion to Source Relations persisted for me, but the Compassion part seemed a little lonesome. Meanwhile, I could Devote myself to what is truly sacred for me, and get to the value in what I'd otherwise call my prideful ways.

The best way for me to share my experience is through my personal polarities. Here they are, minus a few too rare and personal to tell.

Hopeless/Masterful

This was an extreme self-confrontation. My biggest anxieties lie in my battle between unsteadiness and self-defeat, especially around being accomplished at what I am doing while, at the same time, knowing I am masterful and capable of certain forms of self-expression, worthy of certain new maturations as well as being respected. While undergoing this polarity, I witnessed the futility of taking myself so seriously, as well as the social prices I've paid due to so many layers of pride and fear. Time to re-locate my center again.

Equal/"Superior"

I was surprised and elated—and then reassured—to find that the notion of Equality led me to being humble, and the inquiry into

Superiority ended in the fortitude and certainty of being at service. Checks & Balances.

Devotion/Vanity

Here I witnessed the clearest devotion to my spiritual purposes in life, and then the ugly, obsequious taint of pride and complacency within the space of failing source relations. Very straightforward! Dig it!

Safety/Danger

Well before this lab, because I had changed my name a few times within the sight of the social-police, I had rendered myself quite transparent (to me this is an aspect of vertical connection). Meanwhile, being unconsciously pride-driven, I have not wished to explain myself to others, and have made myself scarce (which has allowed some to assume much about me for lack of exposure to me).

Finally, a basic distrust, and dare I say, paranoia, developed in me that has led me not to trust, and to avoid contact much at all with certain persons. Within the space of this polarity in action, I witnessed the translation of my "objective" perception of my "lack-of-trust" into spatial proximity of people actually in the room. It was a leap in perception, from delusion to simple illusion, and then to clarity. Clarity because, when seen as real-time people in proximity, I could no longer generalize to myself that they were untrustworthy. It just didn't work anymore. Then, I was painfully reminded of what I already know all too well: "Define yourself or be defined." Enough said.

The DREAMING RITUAL Lab, Winter 2008
MUSES RITUAL ACTIONS Lab, Winter 2010–2011
Two Lab Reports by Sylvi Alli

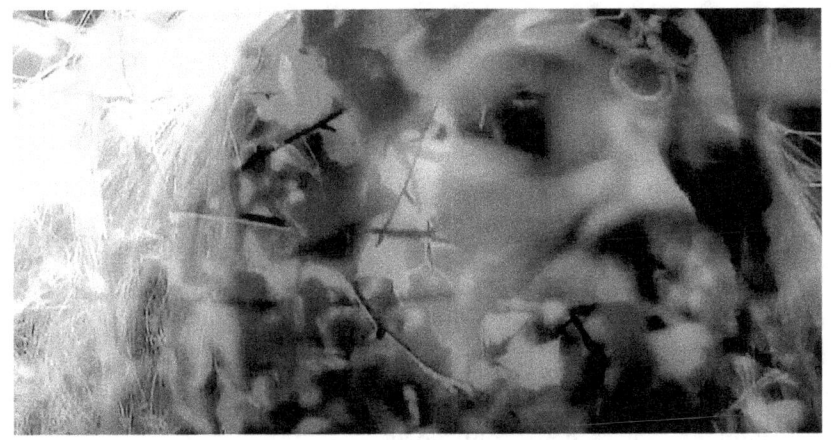

My Third Dreaming Ritual Lab

The winter 2008 session was my third dreaming ritual lab, not to say that the third time is the charm, for that is merely a saying, at best a hope. This time seemed like "getting down to work," somewhat akin to being part of a group of miners piling into the trolley car to be taken down to an honest day's, or in this case, night's work. Because of the large proportion of "newbies" in this lab, there was more emphasis on physical mechanics and embodiment techniques. I experienced this as a valuable opportunity to get more specific—with intention, as well as with my commitment to physical execution. I also believe that the physical emphasis in the particular lab allowed us as a group to enter some rather deep places together, surprising given the number of people new to the paratheatre work here.

In the early stages of working with our dream movements, Antero brought up the importance of distinguishing between "movement" and "activity." It turned out that one of the movements I had chosen to work with, when examined more closely, was actually a combination of several movements that was heavily tied to the activity in the dream from which it appeared. After being encouraged to focus on simple, pure movement (the simpler the movement, the less the tendency to embellish it or stray), I was eventually able to recall five specific movements that I was able to combine in a flowing way to create my personal dream ritual.

When executing our dream rituals through the influences of specific sources, there were always one or two of my movements that stood out as particularly informative to me—whether it was deeper emotional access to the dream, or a stronger awareness of energies in my body, or something beyond words.

This aspect of the dreaming ritual lab—maintaining the integrity of our movements while subjecting them to various sources—stood out to me as the most profound of this lab. Sometimes a source would give my movements a renewed energy, a sense of effortlessness; other times it was like moving deep underwater, slowed down with a quality of heaviness. And then there were times when a completely new level of the movements would be revealed!

A ritual form that was used consistently in this lab was that of exiting the space in No-Form, and reentering the space with the intention of serving what was sacred—each person deciding within themselves what that was. I found this valuable in deepening my sense of self, of what I needed in that moment, and in the serving of what I made sacred, being supported by it throughout the night.

I leave this particular lab with an increased awareness of how the DREAMING is always present—within us, around us—and it is through the deepening of our receptivity, our emptying out, that we are allowed to experience it, to dance it, to tremble in awe of it. And I won't soon forget the moments of unsurpassable beauty that occurred in the room when each of us was totally committed to our ritual movements, serving the sources, serving the DREAMING—so far beyond anything that the mind could choreograph!

Ritual Actions of Muses During Total Lunar Eclipse

Our first session began on the evening of a total lunar eclipse, which ended up playing a part for me in this session. After choosing a trinity to work with in my personal warm-up, I decided to shift it to something more dynamic when we entered the first group ritual. It was an immediate morphing of each component of the original trinity into the forces of Moon, Earth, and Sun (which felt even more charged given the impending Lunar eclipse). Throughout the evening I discovered various aspects of each force, and explored finding movement and sound for each layer that was revealed to me.

After several group rituals exploring our trinities, we moved on to a group ritual of approaching the Muse. Dividing the room into two areas, the first area that we would enter from No-Form was dedicated to the melding and compositing of the three forces of our trinity. The second area was delegated to the realm of the Muses, leaving it unknown whether or not we would encounter the Muse there.

I experienced the first part of the ritual as a merging of parts of myself, specifically using tones that initiated in the belly and the heart and met in the solar plexus where it was directing outwards. The commitment and power of this vocal tone compelled me to enter the Muses' realm.

Immediately upon entering, I had a strong vision of being hooked up somewhere around the heart and solar plexus area with a thin, flexible, clear tube that ran vertically upwards. It was as if the Muse was extracting my "tone" from my body as a pale opalescent liquid. It was not frightening or unpleasant at all, and felt very natural, if a little exciting. Eventually I became aware that I had been transformed into a large, blue, ragged, winged creature. Part of the pattern on my wings appeared slightly illuminated in a dark brilliant blue. All the while I continued my toning, which became a rhythmic pattern of two notes. I remained stationary there until it felt like I had served my purpose, and then I returned to the personal trinity area.

After reconnecting to my trinity, and finding a somewhat quieter merging of the forces, I decided to enter the Muse realm one more time. This time the atmosphere was different, quieter, calmer. It was as if the Muses were resting, hidden somewhere, yet allowing me to visit this foreign landscape—a pale sky, soft hills in the distance. The colors were muted like early morning light. I stood there taking it all in until the vision slowly changed into a blanker, icier version of itself—which I took as my cue to leave.

Both times that I entered and exited the Muse realm, I experienced a strong electrical feeling on the surface of my skin, like supercharged "goose bumps." I returned to the personal trinity area, and collapsed to the floor. I felt done. I slowly stood up, walked over to the No-Form area...decompressing...dissolving.

The MUSES Lab, Spring 2010
Journal Entry by James Wagner, Final Session, April 15th

A Temporary Ending To An Eternal Relationship

These notes were excerpted from a journal kept during a 10-week Muses Lab that met in Berkeley, California in February, March, and April of 2010. What follows are the notes taken after the last of 20 work sessions.

Sequence of tonight's work:

1. *enter space: Space relations.*
2. *access resistance as source, then add back.*
3. *foundation source: verticality.*
4. *warm-up cycle.*

5. *personal trinity: started ocean, mountain, sky. became liquid, solid, vapor/gas in later rituals.*

6. *transition/heat/foundation source jog.*

7. *triangle work. pathways between trinity sources, with Muse source in the middle of the triangle.*

8. *repeat as above, but focusing on approaching the Muse from a variety of entry points along the triangle.*

9. *north/south pass with a gateway. south was designated the creation or construction of the self, and the north was the realm of the Muses, but with the intention of maintaining the self in that space.*

I'm not sure I can put tonight's work into words.

For starters, my experience of verticality tonight was higher and deeper than ever before. I went up to the heat of the sun above, and down to the heat of the Earth's core—to the fire in them both. This was in response to my trinity—ocean, mountain, sky that became earth, water, wind, and also solid, liquid, vapor; as a result, I was looking for the fire, so in this case I ended up finding it in the verticality.

I also found the moon as a cooling source from direct contact with these heat sources, Especially in the space above me—it reminded me of the myth of Icarus, about flying too close to the sun; there is heat and inspiration in that Light as the source of life, but it seems natural to need to cool with the moon and night, to temper the other elements, and to use that heat to forge vessels; using water, earth, and air in alchemical processes, with the heat from above and below always being the catalyst. Something like that...

Also, due to exploring "resistance as source," I learned that I could store energy in resistance. During the triangle work with the trinity of sources, as I moved towards the gateway for "solid" from the heat of the muse source, I realized that resistance was actually stored

Sacred Rites

energy, that it could be used to store energy. For what I'm not sure, but the idea of resistance as storage was an interesting and brand-new notion.

During the final closing circle, as we shared our experiences, there seemed to be a shared group experience of the mundane manifestation of the muses, as if the muses were revealing themselves in daily life, in mundane tasks of the creation of life—even basic self-care rituals, and basic actions that support and lead to larger creative leaps. Also, in my experience, there was a sense of "just so"—that everything was right in the world as it is, that the fire of inspiration was well tempered by the mundane world, and that to fly too close to the sun or for too long is actually not great, that life as it is, the bodies we have, are spirit incarnate, are inspiration given in form.

There was a deep sense of well-being and ease at the end. For me, the whole last ritual was about simple tasks of self-care and self-sustaining tasks: eating, opening doors, washing, etc. Then, when I went to the realm of the muses, it was clearly like a house of worship; their realm was like a church of some kind, a place to come and worship, but still full of small, simple, mundane, gentle tasks. While in that final Muse temple, I also had a notion or experience of making a helmet, but the essence of the experience was just about making artifacts—spiritual artifacts—forms to "hold" or "carry" the energy of spirit. There was a feeling of making it solid, capturing the energy into "resistance" that is form. Something like that.

Many of the actions and gestures in that final ritual in the Realm of the Muses were about ritual actions (communion, hymns, tithing, etc.); they struck me as mundane, and tempered ways to contact Spirit that maintained the self I had created earlier in the ritual. It was a mediated way of contacting Spirit, so as not to rupture this vessel that is James and the form that is James' fairly stable, healthy life. So that felt good—this notion of titrated contact with Pure Spirit, so as not to blow James to smithereens through contact.

Oh, and exploring "communion" turned out to be earth + liquid as the body and blood of the eucharist, and the air/sky part of the trinity turned out to be Song, carrying sound waves on the air as a hymn. So, my trinity returned in the form of religious rites when I was in the realm of Muses.

There was some mention of the notion of "reactivity" in the process, as we were working with the sources. I'm not sure what that was about.

Just as with the first day's arrival of the Muses, the departure of the Muses from the space felt strong, like a goodbye or a finishing of a process. I recall the first day, when we began the work; I could have sworn I physically saw them float in like little orbs of light, little light beings skipping around the upper part of the room, and when we finished our final ritual last night, as all of us stood in No-Form, I again could have sworn I saw the rainbow-colored light-orbs of the Muses lift and depart the space. It was a "taking wing" sort of impression, an ascension perhaps.

That's all for this lab. I am humbled and feel a bit sad tonight, saddened perhaps mostly by my own hubris and offense in relation to the sacred that I got in contact with through the Muses, so I recommit to do better, and bow to you all who may read this at any time.

In Gratitude, James Wagner, April 2010

WEEKEND INTENSIVES
*Outline of Ritual Structures,
Designs, and Methods*
For the ritual facilitator of introductory workshops

From 1977 to 2015, I avoided presenting this work in formats less than four-week Labs, and more often, Labs were presented in durations of two and three months at a time. After relocating from Berkeley and starting over in Portland, the following Weekend Intensive workshop schedule was designed in 2016 as an introduction to the ten-week Labs that culminated in five public productions over the following two years at Linda Austin's PerformanceWorks NW.

In this weekend format, the groups of "newbies" met Saturdays and Sundays from 10am to 4pm on both days. Each day was divided into three parts: 1) 10am to 1pm. 2) 1pm to 1:20pm, snack or light lunch. 3) 1:30pm to 3:30pm, ritual work; 3:30pm to 4pm, ending group circle. This structure and content were subject to change depending on the skills, commitment levels, and talents of each new group. These workshops became an effective way to introduce this work while laying a foundation for long-term Labs. All the page numbers referenced below are from *STATE OF EMERGENCE*, the companion book to *SACRED RITES*.

Saturday

Request silence from the start; no talking once they're inside the workspace. Introduce the idea that this nonverbal process is an experiment, and that at first, there's no right or wrong way to do anything except be open to discovery.

Don't start any inner work until an hour or so into each day's session. Begin very basically, with emphasis on the physical, towards feeling the Body deeply.

...with increasing spatial awareness—such as space forming—moving throughout, and relating with, the space itself as a value. Then, ask the group to explore the workspace to find their own area to claim and own with movements and their energy. Introduce the 5-phase Physical Warm-Up (pp. 61 & 62). After warming up, introduce a Verticality jogging form (pp. 49–55). Then onward into a practice of the No-Form stance (p. 44). Then, move into a group polarity of sources you choose for the group (pp. 65–66). End with the Verticality Ritual (pp. 67–71). Group Circle (ends at 1pm). Suggest a silent break. Group energy drops into feeding and resting, and must be raised again when returning.

1:30pm. Start with one of the Transitory Jogs (p. 64) that leads into resonating tones matching their source. This leads to Foundation Source (p. 51), that transitions into asking the group to find their personal area for the 5-phase physical warm-up (pp. 61 & 62). This leads to a Verticality Jog, and then vocalizing that source. Afterward, send them back to their personal area for a personal polarity of their choice. After this, enter the Human Systems ritual (p. 52) with one side of the room as No-Form, and the rest divided into three zones, each assigned a different bio-system; use 3 systems only—i.e., muscular, skeletal, CNS. End with The 4 Elements ritual (pp. 72–76). Group Circle (ask them to bring three sets of charged polarities for Sunday's session).

Sunday

Standing No-Form practice. Next up, ask them to explore the workspace to find their own area to claim and own with movements and their energy towards the 5-phase Physical Warm-up (pp. 61 & 62). From here, introduce a personal polarity of their choice in their own area. Then onward to the trinity of Head, Heart, Gut, sources in the Body across the floor and back (twice), with emphasis on resonating tones from each source as they move; embodied voice in motion.

Introduce non-directional Jogging. This transitions into a Group Polarity ritual of your choice (pp. 65–66). Group Circle ending (ends at 1pm). Suggest a silent break. Group energy drops into feeding and resting, and must be raised again when returning.

1:30pm. Start with the Rises, 3–5 of them (p. 54), which then leads to Movement stretches (p. 53). This leads to Foundation Source, which transitions into finding their personal area for the 5-phase physical warm-up. After the warm-up, in their own area, ask the group to start a personal polarity of their choice. Then, got to the Verticality Jog around the periphery go the workspace. Suggest a group polarity of your choice (pp. 65–66). From here move into the final ritual of Shadow Work (p. 85–90). Afterward, transition into a No-Form chorus (tight standing circle, facing center) for Verticality choir ritual (p. 56). Group Circle ending.

THE PORTLAND PRODUCTIONS
(2016–2018)
Notes on Pre-Production Labs and Performance Rituals

"Bardoville", "Soror Mystica" reviewed by Oregon ArtsWatch
"The Celebrants" video/review. On approaching a creative state

Living Rituals Dressed Up As Experimental Theatre

"A Turbulence of Muses" (2016)

Five ParaTheatrical ReSearch productions were staged over two years at PerformanceWorks NW in Portland, Oregon. Each one was framed by poetry—*Rimbaud, Bukowski, H.D., Blake, Plath*—presented as oblique narratives to the ritual actions, or as songs, invocations, and sermons, but never as "poetry readings." Each was preceded by a 10-week Lab exploring themes, archetypes, and sources resonant with the poetry. Productions were developed into a living ritual, *spiritual events,* dressed up as experimental theatre. Only one character in each show broke the fourth wall to address the audience directly; the rest remained committed to their internal sources and asocial interplay while ignoring the audience. Each production performed three nights in a row. (Video documents of these productions and others at: verticalpool.com/paratheatre.html.)

"A TURBULENCE OF MUSES"
December 2, 3, & 4, 2016

For Helen, in the virgin shadows and the
impassive radiance in astral silence,
ornamental saps conspired.

Summer's ardour was confided
to silent birds and due indolence
to a priceless mourning boat
through gulfs of dead loves
and fallen perfumes.

After the moment of the woods women's song
to the rumble of the torrent in the ruin of the wood,
of the tinkle of the cowbells to the echo of the vales,
and the cries of the steppes.

For Helen's childhood, furs and shadows trembled,
and the breast of the poor and the legends of heaven.
And her eyes and her dance superior
even to the precious radiance,
to cold influences, to the pleasure of the unique
setting and the unique hour.

"Fairy", by Arthur Rimbaud

Rimbaud

French symbolist poet, Arthur Rimbaud (1854–1891) referred to his creative process as a "systematic disorganization of all the senses" to induce trances and spontaneous visions that inspired the creation of his poetry. Rimbaud's method became our focus for the sources, ritual designs, and characters in *"A Turbulence of Muses"*. I saw this production as a Symbolist ritual, where eight performers represented different dimensions of the poet Rimbaud. There was Raven the Poetic Imagination, Krunk the Inner Critic as Clown, Tubehead the Singing Romantic (and Krunk's paramour), Rimbaud the Dream Ego herself, Three Dreaming Entities, and The Inner Voice who spoke Rimbaud's poetry as a free-floating narrative over the stage action, where the words would drop into different moments in each performance.

Dreaming Ritual Lab

In the pre-production Dreaming Ritual Lab *(State of Emergence,* p. 77), we tapped the sources of dreambody/earthbody, The Four Elements, Nervous/Muscular/Skeletal systems, and the No-form/ Dream/Form continuum. Some of the movement signatures explored by the Dream Ego (Sylvi Alli), and the three Dreamers (Brandt Stickely, Hank Peterson, Memorie Eden) came from movements they recalled from their nocturnal dreams during the Lab.

The Soundscape

Live music was played on a ukelin, a bowed psaltery with zither strings made popular in the 1920's. Meant as a combination of the violin and the Hawaiian ukulele, it lost popularity in the 1970's as it was allegedly too difficult to play. Throughout each of the performances, I improvised all the sounds, tones, melodies, and percussive effects using a violin bow, a pair of small mallets and miked through a mixer with reverb. My objective was to simply provide sonic accents to the unfolding visceral and emotional states embodied by the performers.

"BARDOVILLE"
May 12, 13, 14, 2017

there is enough treachery, hatred violence absurdity
in the average human being to supply any given army
on any given day and the best at murder are those
who preach against it
and the best at hate are those who preach love
and the best at war finally are those who preach peace
those who preach god, need god
those who preach peace do not have peace
those who preach peace do not have love.

                excerpted from *"Genius of the Crowd"*,
                    by Charles Bukowski

Bukowski

Bukowski's crystal clear, uber-realist, confrontational poetry brings fresh perspectives to a vision of societal collapse with no new order yet in sight to replace the old ways. *Bardo* is a Tibetan Buddhist term for an intermediary stage between human incarnations, but also applies to the living who struggle between epochs and eras of their existence. I imagined this *bardo* idea as a setting where three related subsets would interact: 1) a poet performing his work before an audience; 2) seven nonverbal characters embodying the spirits trapped in the words of the Poet, while interacting with each other and the poet, but never the audience; 3) E.V.E., a women's improvisational vocal ensemble invoking sonic atmosphere into the setting. The end of each performance culminated in a **scapegoat ritual** where the poet was sacrificed by the angry spirits—embodied by the performers—that reversed the rage in his words onto himself.

Two-Faced Clowns

Bukowski's poetry brilliantly exposes the corruption resulting from personal and social hypocrisy that must first be faced and owned before creating a new future worth living for. Seven characters were developed during the 10-week, pre-production; 2-Faced Clowns Lab to expose and express personal and collective hypocrisies in extreme characterizations of 2-faced clowns. The workspace floor plan was divided into quarters with each of the four areas representing a different source the clowns would subject themselves to as they physically passed into and through them. This device maintained an ongoing state of transformation and unpredictability for each clown and the

Sacred Rites

group as a whole, resulting in a highly dynamic zone of almost constant interaction.

My personal hypocritical clown was a red-handed Murderous Preacher who randomly selected and speared any clown that I judged sinful. My character was a fusion of the horrific hypocrisy of pedophile priests murdering the innocence of thousands of children, and my own personal Shadow of crushing the spirits of those who opposed or disagreed with me, with proclamations of what I used to dogmatically believe was the truth for all. I have since corrected my evil ways. This was also the only production of the five in Portland that I personally appeared in.

E.V.E. (Experimental Vocal Ensemble)

Musical Director, Sylvi Alli, rehearsed independently with her own group, E.V.E. over ten weeks, developing a series of vocal modalities to draw from when they would improvise vocal creations in the eventual performance. These tonal modes included Eastern European folk melodies, Middle Eastern chants, percussive singing, hymns and hums, whispers and sounds, breath.

The seven performers onstage applied methods for triggering high levels of unpredictability and spontaneous interactions; nothing was choreographed. They also did not relate to, confront, or pay attention to the audience. Those interactions belonged to the Poet who performed his poems to an imaginary audience in his filthy, beer-bottled apartment, while facing the actual audience in the venue. The women of E.V.E. were positioned behind the audience, and offered live vocal creations to the moment-to-moment dynamics onstage as they unfolded.

Review: Bukowski in Bardoville
MITCH RITTER for Oregon ArtsWatch—June 5, 2017

Entering Southeast Portland's Northwest PerformanceWorks studio, the audience for the *Bardoville* premiere finds four women and three men dressed in black, on tape-marked floor quadrants, doing stretching exercises. The audience takes seats in a semi-circle around the bare floor except for a small foldable card table at the front white projection wall with a vintage manual typewriter and empty beer and wine bottles splayed around that small corner littered with balled-up pages of clearly rejected drafts issuing from that typewriter.

High definition video of a graffiti-scrawled freight train crossing a typically beat-down Portland old rail bridge with the clatter and roll sounds amplified to a low rumble are punctuated every few minutes by a clear Tibetan bowl bell from behind the semi-circle seated audience where co-director Sylvi Alli and her three-woman chorus of chant, song and sound vocalizers named E.V.E. (Experimental Vocal Ensemble) assemble around a single microphone.

Their work throughout the nearly hour-long theater ritual will sound at times like wordless harmonic wailing, alternating with liturgical chant that could be coming from a cave or an urban loft where Meredith Monk is vocally composing and de-composing in her own spiritual preparations. At other times, after silent or very low undertone accompaniment or ambient percussion to the archetype interactions, characterizations and movement with poetry unfurled before us, we might hear a lone coyote baying off in the distance or an approaching wolf pack wailing with some subtle phasing and electronic effects. I do hope there will be a CD of the varying three nights of E.V.E. vocal creations made available. Alli's inner ear and her collaborators' willingness to follow her into sonic territories uncharted make for exciting listening whether as accompaniment or focal point.

The Poet (played by Randal S. Slager with no attempt to mimic or impersonate the one and only Bukowski), inhabits the narrative voice quite snugly. His entrance is almost feline, as he slips in from the door with a house cat darting behind from backstage. Dressed in boxer shorts, dark socks, and tank t-shirt, he settles in at the flimsy, folding tv dinner table upon which is perched the vintage manual typewriter. He proceeds to type feverishly at first, then into staccato bursts as the movement characters arise from their stretching positions, and Antero Alli's character of the "Murderous Preacher" peels himself off the front white projection wall where the rumbling freight train had passed, gesturing almost delicately behind the typing Poet with blood-soaked hands.

Like the other six non-verbal and non-named movement actors creating archetypes of their own through paratheatre process sessions, "Murderous Preacher" is dressed in black, but with some golden cross embroidery as the front pattern of his tunic. His head is either hooded, as in a Berber burnoose, or covered in a vaguely papal or perhaps French baker's floppy tri-cornered black chapeau.

The lights go down, the freight train has clattered and rolled on by, and the rear-projection wall reverts to blank while The Poet begins reading from his recently typed and rapidly un-scrolled page the Bukowski words so well chosen for our times

The flow from scene to scene varied in each of the three full-house nights I attended, although the interpretively-perceived scenario retained a narrative integrity around which each character acts and reacts like jazz soloists departing and returning to a melodic structure and interactive core. Sylvi Alli has crafted the musical and aural collage accompaniment with her highly flexible and colorfully timbred chorus to accentuate Bukowski's poetic peculiarities.

Before The Poet has completed his hunt and peck, or yanked another page spared the fate of tossed, balled-up reject, Sylvi Alli and E.V.E. have already begun vocalizing mewling cats getting catty with each other in cramped confines co-habiting with an orally fixated manic-depressive stumblebum in perpetual state of inebriation.

With ritual design and theatrical direction by Antero Alli, *Bardoville* had a narrative arc, and displayed elements of classical tragedy/drama such as confrontation/conflict/resolution. From a relatively restrained opening night, each movement actor inhabiting an archetype became more expressive and less inhibited or confined to their energy quadrant.

Wendy Allegaert's physicalizing of her Angel/Witch duality archetype, and her blossoming from opening night to closing night felt especially nuanced, contrasting with Hank Peterson's "Orphaned Rock Star" persona that was developed within the ensemble rather sublimely, and expressing his character's facets the first two nights while going full primal scream on closing night. Peterson's background in modern Japan's *Butoh* theater, with its paradoxical forces of seeking to preserve tradition and ritual while being authentic to a world that undermines tradition and ritual the more one seeks to cling to or fetishize these identity tokens felt utterly raw in its activist release of conflicting impulses. From pagan to Public Servant to vigilante, Peterson's sublimation during the takedown of The Poet developed incrementally until it blew and spewed all over.

Four-part unison whistling segueing into Balkan polyphonic harmonizing, Sylvi Alli and E.V.E. created a soundscape that exceeded the sonic challenges of largely non-verbal paratheater. Her arrangement of the closing round, "In the Belly of the Beast" by the Bay Area's Peter Elman, brought it all home with comfort rather than terror.

"SOROR MYSTICA"
Ritual Invocation of the Anima
December 1, 2, 3, 2017

When in the company of the gods,
I loved and was loved,
never was my mind stirred
to such rapture,
my heart moved
to such pleasure,
as now, to discover
over Love, a new Master:
His, the track in the sand
from a plum-tree in flower
to a half-open hut-door,
(or track would have been
but wind blows sand-prints from the sand,
whether seen or unseen):
His, the Genius in the jar
which the Fisherman finds,
He is Mage, bringing myrrh.

from *"The Walls Do Not Fall"*,
by Hilda Doolittle (aka H.D.)

H.D.

Hilda Doolittle (aka HD) wrote *"The Walls Do Not Fall"* (the first of part in her *Trilogy*), in London during the 1942 Nazi blitzkrieg air strikes. Sheltered underground, she composed *Trilogy* as bomb after bomb exploded over the city above her. I was deeply inspired by her indomitable spirit during that era of unspeakable strife, tragedy, and warfare, and chose nine stanzas from *"The Walls Do Not Fall"* for its oracular visions of death and rebirth, her words so finely crafted as if carved in bone.

The Anima

The Anima archetype—that wild, erotic, and anarchic dimension of the Holy Feminine possessing, vexing, seducing, and inspiring artists since the beginning of Time—demands to be related with. She will not be ignored! My own courtship with the Anima (She is not "my" Anima; She belongs to no one!) has been partly sustained by love letters composed to Her (some call them poems).

Temple of the Divine Feminine

Four women, dressed in off-white from head to toe, remained within a large, triangular temple-space, bordered by candles at each corner dedicated to a different source of the Divine Feminine: Creator, Destroyer, and Nourisher. Their ongoing ritual worship of the Divine Feminine expressed itself through constant surrender to these three sources. A fifth character, Aether, dressed from head to toe in black, acted as their guardian who also monitored the Alchemist who kept sneaking into the temple to observe the women.

'Soror Mystica': Breaking the Frame
ParaTheatrical ReSearch's ritualistic production is and isn't a performance.
Matthew Neil Andrews review, Oregon ArtsWatch
December 3, 2017

I remember seeing Grotowski's indelible name in connection with Antero Alli, perpetrator of tonight's performance, and my mind goes to Artaud and Brecht. They started warming up on the dance floor before they even opened the doors. We join our story already in progress. I take a seat, then another. My boots squeak, the floor creaks, I feel terrible for interrupting the performance. What performance? They're just warming up. A static image of some kind of medieval amphitheater enlivens the screen behind the dancers, bracketed by bare branches hanging over candles on columns at the edge of the dance floor. Music that sounds more or less like Hildegard's plays over the speakers. People trickle in. They keep silent. They prepare themselves physically and spiritually—as I have—for the Work which is about to commence.

A bell rings out from the back of the room, its rich tone brought forth by a semi-hidden percussionist crouching serenely back by the sound board, and the quintet of dancers changes the routine, getting more active, and changing directions and the flow of their movements and breathing exercises. This happens four or five times, and eventually the show starts. The last guests arrive, talking rather loudly, unsure of what they're getting into. They stagger down the dark hallway defined by the stage's curtained edge, and when I see the fella's big fakey-fake beard, I realize I've been had again. Damn that frame. Damn it to Hell.

Fakey Beard Fella (The Alchemist, L.D. McClure) and his Guide, a Dark Woman straight out of Shakespeare (The Sorceress, Greeta Ahart), proceed to the center of the stage, where they exchange a series of alchemical keywords ("Earth," "Putrefaction," "Energy," "Transubstantiation") as if they're having a normal, expressive conversation. When the alchemist and the witch seat themselves at the table off to the edge of the stage, and begin to watch the same show I am—while still being part of it—I realize that "ritual" means going both below and above the normal realm of mesocosmic narrative.

Conventional theater (and movies, novels, etc.) is concerned with relatable things like real-world characters, dialogue, plot, and so on. Ritualistic narrative, by contrast, concerns itself with little, repeated details like the keyword exchange (repeated throughout the remainder of the performance), and large-scale formal elements outlining the procedures of the rite. Microcosm and macrocosm. Consider the grand symbolisms and millions of little jokes that characterize a movie like, say, Jodorowsky's *Holy Mountain*.

In *"Soror Mystica"*, the large-scale form follows the transmutation of the alchemist through the (inter)action of the four elements—each endowed with their own agency, each enacting their own rituals, not subservient to the alchemist, but welcoming him into their temple—and the masked shadow-man who dwells at the threshold and drives the querent's transfiguration. All of this further fractures the frame, because we see these people both as actors (that fake fucking beard!) enacting a rite, and as the incorporeal substances and energies which they are, for the next hour or so, embodying. The miraculous thing about all of this is the performers are openly working for their own benefit.

Alli's own ParaTheatrical ReSearch Mission Statement reads, in part: "This work provides performers a safe space to expose and correct whatever habits may be crimping their talents, to non-performers seeking greater access to creative states embodied in presence, movement, and vocalization." This is not a performance, except that it absolutely is.

With me so far? One last layer: while Sylvi Alli and Amma Li Grace make spare, percussive music from the back, Nita Bryant's disembodied voice (The Oracle) reads poetry. Not something overtly alchemical, and not something hip and chaos magicky like I might have expected from Alli, but poetry by one of my favorite Pennsylvanian expatriates, H.D. aka Hilda Doolittle. The lines all come from "The Walls Do Not Fall", the first part of H.D.'s majestic *Trilogy*, composed in London while she wrote against the Blitz in the apartment she shared with her lover Bryher. The mark of war is there, sure, but more important is the defiant transmutation of violence that marks the true spiritual work.

Sacred Rites

The Oracle intones:

>be firm in your own small, static, limited
>orbit and the shark-jaws of outer circumstance
>will spit you forth: be indigestible, hard, ungiving,
>so that, living within, you beget, self-out-of-self,
>selfless,
>that pearl-of-great-price.
>And:
>Let us, however, recover the Sceptre, the rod of power:
>it is crowned with the lily-head or the lily-bud:
>it is Caduceus; among the dying it bears healing:
>or evoking the dead, it brings life to the living.
>
>>from "*Trilogy*", by H.D.

More, I am forbidden say. I can reveal that everyone there seemed moved and a bit confused, as if the story's deepest meanings had slipped in past everyone's conscious monitors, and performed some manner of psychic cleansing. My own feelings were somewhere between the endorphin high of a good long walk, and the theta waves that characterize float-tank experiences. I did hear a lot of nervous, uncertain, satisfied, relieved, good-natured chuckles mixed through the final applause, and throughout the performance a woman in front of me couldn't stop giggling. I was enjoying the Hell out of it all.

"FALLEN MONSTERS"
May 11, 12, 13, 2018

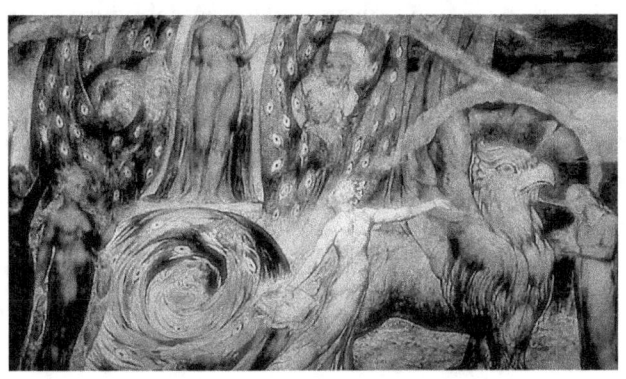

Dear Mother, dear Mother, the Church is cold,
But the Ale-house is healthy & pleasant & warm;
Besides I can tell where I am use'd well,
Such usage in heaven will never do well.

But if at the Church they would give us some Ale.
And a pleasant fire, our souls to regale;
We'd sing and we'd pray, all the live-long day;
Nor ever once wish from the Church to stray,

Then the Parson might preach & drink & sing.
And we'd be as happy as birds in the spring:
And modest dame Lurch, who is always at Church,
Would not have bandy children nor fasting nor birch.

And God like a father rejoicing to see,
His children as pleasant and happy as he:
Would have no more quarrel with the Devil or the Barrel
But kiss him & give him both drink and apparel.

"The Little Vagabond", by William Blake

Blake

William Blake (1757–1827) was largely unrecognized during his lifetime, though he is now considered a seminal figure in the history of poetry and visual arts of the Romantic Age (1800 to 1850). During his adult life he was dismissed as a lunatic, enduring countless rejections and betrayals from the local society that forced him into isolation and depression. Yet he never stopped creating art, poetry, and the illuminated manuscripts that combined both into a new art form. At the time of his death, his illuminated book, *Songs of Innocence & Experience* had sold only 30 copies! And yet, he kept creating! "Fallen Monsters" celebrates the resiliency of the Creative Spirit in Blake and in all committed artists to survive the onslaughts of persecution, trauma, and other hellacious attempts to oppress the joy of creation.

The Contract Lab

This Lab was dedicated to rituals that exposed patterns of oppression to the creative spirit by threats of shaming, blaming, ridicule, abuse, and over-judgmentalism of the self and/or of others. Once exposed, these threats were defused by setting up a contract between the Child and the Adult functions of the Self, where the Adult had to earn the trust of the Child as a protector; rituals were designed to enact and support this contract. When the Adult oppresses the joy of creation, it triggers a spectrum of reactions within the Child who sees that Adult as a monster. This Adult/Child contract was extended into the creation of handmade monster-masks for the Children to play monsters for each other in the performances of *Fallen Monsters*.

Musical Director, Sylvi Alli, set eight of Blake's *Songs of Innocence & Experience* to song, accompanying herself on accordion. A film collage of Blake's visionary art was projected onscreen while she sang these songs to the ritual actions onstage. For my spoken and unseen role as the Voice of Oppression, I announced amplified "demonic mantras" from behind the audience: OBEY THE RULES! YOU ARE NOT ENOUGH! YOU DON'T FIT IN! SHUT UP! The performers, as Children, discovered their most honest reactions to these oppressive messages, and then moved on towards discovering the eternal delight of creation.

None of the characters broke the fourth wall and related directly to the audience except two of the Children (Patton Small and Lindsay Reich), who ended each performance with a dramatic recital of Blake's "The Human Abstract":

Pity would be no more,
If we did not make somebody Poor;
And Mercy no more could be,
If all were as happy as we;
And mutual fear brings peace;
Till the selfish loves increase.

Then Cruelty knits a snare,
And spreads his baits with care.
He sits down with holy fears,
And waters the ground with tears;
Then Humility takes its root
Underneath his foot.

Soon spreads the dismal shade
Of Mystery over his head;
And the Caterpillar and Fly,
Feed on the Mystery.

And it bears the fruit of Deceit,
Ruddy and sweet to eat,
And the Raven his nest has made
In its thickest shade.

The Gods of the earth and sea,
Sought thro' Nature to find this Tree
But their search was all in vain;
There grows one in the Human Brain.

"The Human Abstract", by William Blake

"ESCAPE FROM CHAPEL PERILOUS"
November 29 & 30, December 1 & 2, 2018

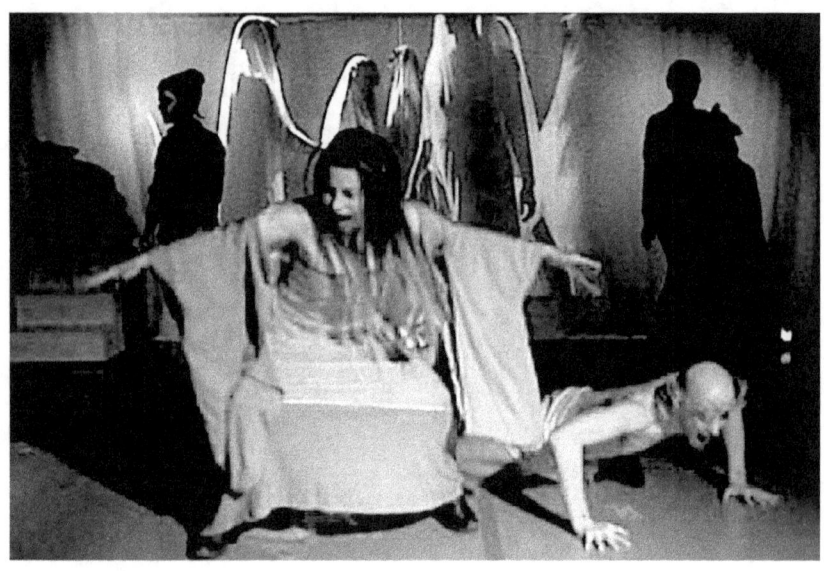

In the marketplace they are piling the dry sticks.
A thicket of shadows is a poor coat. I inhabit
The wax image of myself, a doll's body.
Sickness begins here: I am the dartboard for witches.
Only the devil can eat the devil out.
In the month of red leaves I climb to a bed of fire.

It is easy to blame the dark: the mouth of a door,
The cellar's belly. They've blown my sparkler out.
A black-sharded lady keeps me in parrot cage.
What large eyes the dead have!
I am intimate with a hairy spirit.
Smoke wheels from the beak of this empty jar.

If I am a little one, I can do no harm.
If I don't move about, I'll knock nothing over. So I said,
Sitting under a potlid, tiny and inert as a rice grain.
They are turning the burners up, ring after ring.
We are full of starch, my small white fellows. We grow.
It hurts at first. The red tongues will teach the truth.

Mother of beetles, only unclench your hand:
I'll fly through the candle's mouth like a singeless moth.
Give me back my shape. I am ready to construe the days
I coupled with dust in the shadow of a stone.
My ankles brighten. Brightness ascends my thighs.
I am lost, I am lost, in the robes of all this light.

"Witch Burning", by Sylvia Plath

Plath

Sylvia Plath's poetry illuminates the darker recesses of the psyche—*the despair, the horrors of unbearable truths*—with uncommon elegance and beauty. It was an obvious direction to accompany our ritual exploration of the Chapel Perilous metaphor symbolizing the dark night of the soul. I chose to frame her poetry (from her *"Crossing the Water"* series) as **sermons** delivered by Father Timeless—the resident priest of this chapel—to the audience as the imaginary congregation. Other characters did not relate with the audience directly until the very end. These were the four Lost Souls projected out of their living human bodies that performed repetitive rituals of obsession until their eventual escape and return to embodiment.

Other characters included two recently deceased Buddhist monks who arrived in the Chapel as their *bardo* between incarnations. Two statues in the chapel, Trickster Jesus and Mad Mary (who sang), came to life and taunted the Lost Souls when the priest was not looking. A fourth Preview night was added to allow development in this, our most complex production.

The Labyrinth Archetype

The Labyrinth represents a spiritual journey through the internal landscape—its secret chambers and rooms, its spiral pathways and corridors, many leading to dead ends with few escapes from the complex weave of Psyche. The 10-week, pre-production Labyrinth Lab explored multiple internal sources through solo and group rituals of worship, repetition, and escape. In addition to our practice of paratheatre methods, I introduced a pantomime technique for creating the illusion of opening and closing imaginary doors with the four women portraying the Lost Souls. Near the end of the production they would repeatedly apply this technique to appear as if they were passing through multiple doors on their way somewhere. Eventually they broke the fourth wall and stepped into the audience before quickly exiting the building. BLACK OUT.

THE CELEBRANTS
A Paratheatrical Video Experiment

In January of 2023, I came up with an idea for a 32-minute video set in three parts to show something of how I experience the creative process—from ideation, to discussion, to performance. Since most of my approach to creative states over the last forty years has developed through my experiences in the group ritual dynamics of Paratheatre, this experiment had to unfold organically and not appear staged or "instructional." *The Celebrants* is about three performing artists— Sylvi Alli, singer; Douglas Allen, dancer; and myself on electric guitar—who meet in Sylvi's and my home to address the question "How do you enter a creative state?" And then, based on our responses, we launch into spontaneous performance.

We had no idea, or interest for that matter, in how it would turn out, or look like, or sound like. We were experimenting with an alternative idea of improvisation, born from the Paratheatre method called asocial interplay defined by a state of mutual offering of the self, rather than tapping the energy of others to animate self-expression. The following film review by David Finkelstein articulates this process better than I can and that's why it's included here.

FILM REVIEW
by David Finkelstein, Lake Ivan Film Journal
June 6, 2023

The Celebrants is Antero Alli's latest documentation of his lifelong paratheatrical research: the use of vocal and movement improvisation, normally thought of as artistic tools, as a method of spiritual and emotional exploration for its own sake (which also happens to produce some fascinating performances along the way, as a kind of artistic by-product).

The 32-minute film is a documentation of a workshop in which Alli, his partner Sylvi Alli, and collaborator Douglas Allen gather together in the Alli's home, discussing the focus and motivation for

Sacred Rites

their creative work, and then launch into an extended improvisation, with Sylvi's wordless vocalizations, Antero's processed guitar sounds, and Douglas' movement improvisation. The captivating opening sequence of the film shows a domestic scene, with Douglas apparently a house-guest at the Alli's, sleeping on the couch, while Sylvi plays Debussy on the piano and Antero goes over his notes. Sylvi and Douglas erupt into a playful, spontaneous moment of vocal and bodily improvisation in the kitchen, while preparing tea.

Art-making is usually seen as a highly specialized form of work, bracketed from daily life, but here it is depicted as fully integrated with the quotidian. This holistic approach prepares us for the notion that performance techniques can encompass both art-goals and life-goals.

Over cups of tea, Antero asks his collaborators how they enter a creative state: finding a place within themselves where creativity is able to flow forth spontaneously and easily, and he listens intently as they give their answers (both of which are well worth studying). Antero outlines his vision of their project: he sees it as a form of group improvisation which is structured quite differently from what performing artists usually think of as "improv."

Whereas a typical "improv" one might see from a comedy group or an experimental jazz group would involve trading ideas and riffs back and forth, bouncing impulses around a group, with energy being generated primarily from "horizontal" interactions among the artists, he is proposing that each of the three of them generate the energy for the work from more "vertical" sources, that is, wellsprings of archetypal energies which are available at all times to human beings, accessible through the gateways of the body and the nervous system. (He doesn't use exactly this terminology in the film; I'm borrowing here from his earlier films and books.) Each of the three participants allows themselves to be filled with these energies, which then spill over into actual sounds and movements.

The remainder of the film is a documentation of the improvisation itself, using somewhat grainy black and white footage, and skillfully superimposing images of dancer, singer and guitarist. The three artists brilliantly do exactly what they said they would do: allowing themselves to be filled with energies from deep within the body, and then "offering" this energy to the other two. Sylvi's haunting vocalizations sound animal at times, a cross between birds and wolves, veering between pitched and un-pitched passages of music, while Antero creates walls of texture, not clearly tonal, and Douglas' movements resemble something between martial arts, and motions in which he appears to be digging, searching, drifting through space.

Sacred Rites

They do indeed affect one another: Sylvi's singing eventually lines up precisely into the meter and key of Antero's guitar, and Douglas' movements become rhythmically aligned as well, but it is more a case of their three energies throwing "sparks" across the space, finding mutual nodes of resonance, moments where their energies align in frequency, rather than by self-consciously tossing riffs back and forth like a ball. In certain sequences, footage of Douglas dancing from two different moments in the improv are superimposed, and this serves to reinforce the impression of the "vertical" nature of the sources for this work.

The Celebrants manages to perfectly balance its three centers of interest: *Theory, Practice, and Life*. The improvisation itself is such a compelling act of spontaneous creation, full of hauntingly beautiful moments and miraculous interconnections, that I had to both respect and celebrate the combination of artistic skill and self-knowledge that allows these three individuals to find such depth of expression and to bring it spectacularly to life. By eschewing a superficial approach to "finding connections," these three artists are able to connect with one another at a very deep level, underneath the individual sounds and movements, in a place from which human consciousness is born. The practice embodies the theory, and both of them embody the art of living. It's a vision of a fully integrated mode of being which is not simply a cause for celebration, it *is* celebration.

Watch THE CELEBRANTS
verticalpool.com/celebrants.html

About the Author

Antero Alli is the author of esoteric books such as Experiential Astrology, The Eight-Circuit Brain, The Akashic Record Player, Angel Tech, State of Emergence, Towards an Archeology of the Soul, Last Words, and other titles. A prolific underground filmmaker, he is the founder and artistic director of ParaTheatrical ReSearch. You can find more about Antero at:

verticalpool.com/us.html

MORE TITLES FROM ANTERO ALLI

ANGEL TECH
A Modern Shaman's Guide to Reality Selection

Angel Tech is a comprehensive compendium of insights and techniques for the direct application of Timothy Leary's Eight-Circuit Brain model for Intelligence Increase. What Dr. Leary posited as theory and Dr. Robert Anton Wilson brilliantly demonstrated in sociopolitical, mathematical and intellectual proofs, Antero Alli has extended into tangible tasks, exercises, rituals and meditations.

THE EIGHT-CIRCUIT BRAIN
Navigational Strategies for the Energetic Body

The Eight-Circuit Brain advances and expands the material presented in *Angel Tech,* a compendium of techniques and practical applications based on Timothy Leary's 8-Circuit Brain model. After more than twenty years of research and experimentation, Antero's earlier findings are significantly updated and enriched.

MORE TITLES FROM ANTERO ALLI

STATE OF EMERGENCE
Experiments in Group Ritual Dynamics

State of Emergence presents a group ritual technology for gaining access to impulses, emotions and sensations through movement, vocalization and action. This somatic work explores a dynamic visceral interpretation of C.G. Jung's 'active imagination' for making the Unconscious, conscious that can enrich any ritual, dance and theatre practice as well as anyone ready to start their own creative ritual group for self-discovery.

EXPERIENTIAL ASTROLOGY
From the Map to the Territory

Experiential Astrology revisions the horoscope as a map to access the autonomous forces represented by the planetary symbols and the twelve archetypes of the zodiac. By changing the traditional terms of 'planets, houses and signs' to 'Forces, States and Styles', the author invites you on a journey to discover the very heart of the human condition. Features interpretive techniques culled from over thirty years of astrological study and practice.

MORE TITLES FROM ANTERO ALLI

THE AKASHIC RECORD PLAYER
A Non-Stop Geomantic Conspiracy

Based on a true story, inspired by the author's unexpected 7th circuit activation (ref: Leary's 8-Circuit Brain model), and his attempt to integrate these mystical experiences with the help of people he met on his journey back from "the center of the earth." A story about miraculous interactions, sifted through a mythic, allegorical context. Myth is the very language of life, and through its articulation, we become more alive.

THE BIG BLACK BOOK
Become Who You Are
With Christopher S. Hyatt & friends

Most sections of *The Big Black Book* were written by Christopher S. Hyatt along with his friends and colleagues between 2003 and 2008, and were originally published as individual booklets. Now the entire series has been collected into this single volume. But what is *The Big Black Book* about? Little more can be said lest we give away its intent and reduce its impact.

MORE TITLES FROM ANTERO ALLI

A MODERN SHAMAN'S GUIDE TO A PREGNANT UNIVERSE

With Christopher S. Hyatt, Ph.D.

The Pregnant Universe is a Neural Cocktail party of a brain getting drunk on itself. It is the essence of slimy copulation between known and unknown forces. As the planet braces for a series of new contractions, bizarre and interesting forces are being born—brains with new centers, new chemicals, new visions—going far beyond the suited dinosaurs prattling their slogans.

REBELS & DEVILS
The Psychology of Liberation

Contributions by Antero Ali, Wm. S. Burroughs, Timothy Leary, Robert Anton Wilson, Aleister Crowley, A.O. Spare, Jack Parsons, Genesis P-Orridge, and many, many others.

"When he put the gun to my head at 16 I left home..." So begins this remarkable book which brings together some of the most talented, controversial and rebellious people *ever*. Not to be missed!

MORE TITLES FROM ANTERO ALLI

PARATHEATRE
A Ritual Technology for Self-Initiation

Since 1977, Antero Alli has developed a ritual technology for Self-Initiation—Paratheatre—combining techniques of theatre, dance and zazen to access and express the internal landscape. Paratheatre is highly transformative, and has served as a critical source of inspiration for many of Antero's artistic endeavors, especially his films. (Audio)

8-CIRCUITS OF CONSCIOUSNESS

In this video, Antero Alli discusses his research results and a wide variety of perceptions on Timothy Leary's 8-Circuit Brain model for Intelligence Increase. Antero introduces the origin of this system, and how his interpretations differ from Dr. Leary's and Robert Anton Wilson's, along with his insights on the vertical connectivities between upper and lower circuits, the function and nature of shock, the first and second attentions, and much, much more. (Video)

MORE TITLES FROM ANTERO ALLI

TO DREAM OF FALLING UPWARDS

The elder Magus just passed away. Jack Mason, a promising young sex magickian cultivated to advance the lineage, loses it all when the elder Magus' biological son unexpectedly inherits everything with plans to commercialize and franchise the Temple. Jack plots deadly revenge and falls into a dizzying maze of encounters with underworld characters, desert brujas, and a twist of fate he never saw coming…or did he? (Video)

UNDER A SHIPWRECKED MOON

The power of a long-dead family secret is unleashed when the rituals of a self-made shamanic punk rocker catapult him into the spirit realm in search of his father, a ship's captain who drowned at sea. Meanwhile, back in the real world, he and his family gather around the bedside of his grandfather who has suddenly reappeared after a fifteen-year absence. A surrealistic fable of love, giant hedgehogs, and the mystical depths of family bonds. (Video)

THE *Original* FALCON PRESS

Invites You to Visit Our Website:
originalfalcon.com

At our website you can:

- Browse the online catalog of all of our great titles
- Find out what's available and what's out of stock
- Get special discounts
- Order our titles through our secure online server
- Find products not available anywhere else including:
  – One of a kind and limited availability products
  – Special packages
  – Special pricing
- Get free gifts
- Join our email list for advance notice of New Releases and Special Offers
- Find out about book signings and author events
- Send email to our authors
- Read excerpts of many of our titles
- Find links to our authors' websites
- Discover links to other weird and wonderful sites
- And much, much more

Get online today at originalfalcon.com

www.ingramcontent.com/pod-product-compliance
Lightning Source LLC
Chambersburg PA
CBHW070055080526
44586CB00013B/1066